HEBREWS
A Commentary

DAVID M. LEVY

HEBREWS
A Commentary

DAVID M. LEVY

The Friends of Israel Gospel Ministry, Inc.

HEBREWS
A Commentary

by David M. Levy

Copyright © 2015 by The Friends of Israel Gospel Ministry, Inc.
Bellmawr, NJ 08099

First Printing. 2015

ISBN-9780915540105
Library of Congress Control Number: 2014950311

Table of Contents

PREFACE

The book of Hebrews ranks as one of the most important epistles in the New Testament. It presents Jesus Christ as the divine Son of God, with convincing arguments that prove Jesus fulfills the Messianic Hope anticipated by Jewish people for centuries.

It also presents a masterful, systematic treatment of Christ's supremacy and sufficiency that is unparalleled in other books of the New Testament Canon. It reveals Christ's superiority over angels, Moses, and the Aaronic priesthood and reveals how Christ's sacrificial death on the cross provided a better rest for believers, mediated a better New Covenant, abrogated the Old Testament Levitical system, and secured a better way of faith and practice for all who trust in Him as Savior.

The message is delivered in sermonic style. It is filled with exhortations, warnings, and encouragement directed specifically toward Jewish believers. Some such believers, who were immature in their spiritual lives, are exhorted to grow in the knowledge of God's Word and strive toward spiritual maturity.

Other Jewish believers, who were suffering severe persecution, are encouraged not to renounce their profession of Jesus as Messiah but to continue in their commitment to Him. They were on the verge of returning to Judaism, with its laws and ceremonial rituals. By studying and applying God's Word, they could become strong in their new faith and able to withstand persecution from those who opposed belief in Christ.

Hebrews also explains that if professing believers refuse to heed the author's warnings, they will experience divine chastening or even suffer judgment from God the Father.

In order to encourage these new believers, the author presented portraits of Old Testament men and women who believed the unseen and trusted in God's promises. They waited patiently for the promises to come to fruition, rarely seeing them fulfilled. These saints refused to allow persecution, pain, prison, or peril weaken their faith. They rose above disappointment, depression, discouragement, distrust, and even the threat of death, allowing none of these factors to dampen their devotion to God.

Speaking like a pastor, the author treated believers as disciples and instructed them on the moral and ethical issues of the Christian life. He emphasized that what they claim to believe about God should be manifested in their daily relationships with believers and nonbelievers alike. And he provided wise counsel to Christians on the subjects of compassion, chasteness, contentment, consistency, commitment, and consecration to the Lord.

Hebrews exhorts believers never to stop reflecting on the ministries and conduct of their leaders who are now with the Lord, whose lives and preaching greatly influenced them and laid the foundation for their commitment to Christ. Christians are called on to imitate carefully the faith of these departed leaders. But above all, they are to remember and imitate their supreme Leader, Jesus Christ, because He is "the same yesterday, today, and forever" (Heb. 13:8).

The epistle's conclusion gives a final exhortation to believers, encouraging them to persevere to spiritual maturity. The exhortation focuses on Christ's shed blood, His resurrection, and the New Covenant blessing He secured.

It is my prayer that your study of Hebrews will provide spiritual enlightenment and encouragement in your earthly pilgrimage of faith and give you a greater appreciation of Christ's supremacy and sufficiency. The insights presented in Hebrews, if applied to your life, will strengthen your resolve to grow and mature in Christ.

As you personally apply the many lessons and exhortations in the book of Hebrews, may you, too, renew your commitment to serve our precious Lord.

INTRODUCTION
TO THE BOOK OF HEBREWS

The book of Hebrews stands out as a masterpiece of revelation from God. It is one of the most significant books in the Canon of Scripture, filling a great gap within the New Testament and, in a wonderful way, providing the link between the dispensations of the Old and New Testaments. The revelation in the book of Hebrews provides insight into how to interpret many prophecies in the Hebrew Scriptures that were shrouded in mystery but are now unveiled through Jesus Christ. The book explains many of the cardinal doctrines of the Christian faith, giving believers a solid foundation on which to grow in Christ.

The Epistle to the Hebrews also uniquely presents the person and work of Jesus Christ. It deals especially with theological issues concerning His incarnation, priesthood, testing, faith, endurance, substitutionary death, resurrection, New Covenant ministry, and advocacy in heaven for all believers. Crowned in heaven with glory and honor, Christ is the ultimate authority as the divine Son of God manifested in the flesh and is superior to all the angelic host of heaven, as well as to Abraham, Moses, Joshua, and the Levitical priests.

Hebrews differs from other New Testament epistles in three ways: First, there is no salutation. The author immediately launched into the subject of who Christ is and how He is superior in His person and ministry. Second, Hebrews is shrouded in anonymity as to its author and addressees, and it provides no information concerning when and where it was written. Third, it concludes with an emotional challenge, urging readers to become complete in Christ.

The book weaves together exposition and exhortation in a sermonic tone of doctrine and practical application. Hebrews is divided into two major sections: doctrinal (1:1—10:18) and personal and practical (10:19—13:25). The doctrinal section contrasts Old Testament revelation with New Testament revelation. In the Old Testament, God spoke "at various times and in various ways . . . in time past to the fathers by the prophets," giving revelation to Israel in the Law, historical books, and the prophets (1:1). In the New Testament, God "has in these last days spoken to us by His Son [Jesus Christ the Son of God]" (v. 2). In other words, God's revelation to the Old Testament prophets was only partial and periodic. From the time of Adam to the prophet Malachi, God progressively revealed His plan, program, and purposes. Old Testament revelation set the stage for unveiling the sufficiency and superiority of Jesus Christ. The preeminent revelation was to come through Jesus Christ who would not only speak *for* God but *as* God Himself. Hebrews states succinctly that God "has in these last days spoken to us by His Son" (v. 2). That is, Jesus Christ will interpret and explain the works and will of God the Father. Thus the New Testament is far more glorious than the Old.

The practical section, building on the knowledge of doctrine, presents the type of life every believer is to live—one of faith, hope, love, and total commitment to Christ. Putting the doctrinal and practical together, the epistle warns readers continually not to live in sin; not to be slothful in their commitments; and, above all, not to leave the Christian faith.

Author

The book's human author is unknown. The epistle provides no indication of his identity, nor does it provide the information necessary to deduce his identity through circumstances or connections with other people. The question of who wrote the book of Hebrews has been debated from the epistle's inception.

The writing indicates that the author possessed a highly skilled literary competency and was proficient in classical Greek. Numerous suggestions have surfaced throughout church history as to whether he was an apostle or someone closely associated with an apostle. However, there has been little agreement within the church. It is certain he was a Christian in the first century because Clement of Rome spoke of the epistle as early as A.D. 95.

Mentioned as possible authors are Paul, Luke, Barnabas, Silas, Philip, and Apollos. Many conservative scholars lean toward Paul or someone close to Paul (possibly Luke). Yet other conservative scholars argue convincingly that Paul was not the author, based on style, vocabulary, and lack of identity (not characteristic of Paul's writings).

The text does prompt certain conclusions about the writer: He was a second-generation Christian (2:3). He had a thorough knowledge of the Old Testament and Jewish tradition (1:1). He must have been Jewish or close to the history, traditions, and institutions of Judaism. And, finally, if the author was not Paul, he was extremely close to Paul and associated with people in Paul's circle, such as Timothy (13:23).

To prove authorship is beyond the scope of this discussion. However, a recommended reading list at the back of this book provides the necessary materials for research on the subject, if anyone is so inclined.

It would seem, from all indication and for whatever reason, the author wanted to remain anonymous. In the final analysis, we do not know who wrote the book of Hebrews.

Approximate Date

Although the date of Hebrews is not stated within the epistle, it is possible to narrow the date to within a few years., The epistle could not have been written after A.D. 95 because Clement (the bishop of Rome) quoted from Hebrews; nor could it have been written after A.D. 70 because there is no mention of the second Temple and Jerusalem being destroyed by Rome. Surely, the sacrificial system within the Temple was still operative; if it had not been, the author would have mentioned that it had already ceased, but he did not (see 8:4, 13; 9:6–9; 10:1–3).

There were two Roman persecutions before A.D. 70: one under Claudius (A.D. 49), and one under Nero (A.D. 64). Hebrews 10:32–34 mentions a great persecution within this time period (cf. Acts 18:2). As mentioned earlier, the letter was written during the second generation of Christians (Heb. 2:1–4), sometime after the salvation of the people being addressed (5:12). They had forgotten their former days (10:32), and some of their leaders had already died (13:7). Timothy, however, was still alive (v. 23). They had not yet died for their faith (12:4), but the day was approaching when Judaism would be shaken to its foundation (v. 27). Most likely the book was written sometime during the late 50s or early 60s A.D.

Addressees

The epistle was clearly written to a specific group of Jewish believers whom the author knew well (cf. 13:18–19, 23–24). The gospel was first preached to the Jewish people in Jerusalem (Rom. 1:16; Acts 2—3; 7). Thousands of them had accepted Jesus as the Messiah and immediately began to propagate the gospel message they had received. Jewish people constituted the Christian church for at least 15 years before the gospel went to the Gentiles.

Hebrews addresses the second generation of Jewish believers (Heb. 2:3–4), many of whom were still babes in Christ (5:11–14). Some had compromised their faith and were considering a return to Judaism (10:23–25). Others had already dropped out of the Christian community. The epistle encourages these believers to go on to maturity in Christ (6:1–2).

In addressing the abandonment of their new faith, the author boldly proclaimed that Jesus Christ is superior to anything Judaism could ever offer them. The Word counsels these believers to anchor their faith in Him who is the same yesterday, today, and forever; follow the faith of their godly leaders; and not be tossed about with false doctrines that would lead them away from Christ (Heb. 13:7–9, 17).

The author closed his epistle with a final prayer and pronouncement of blessing and benediction. God had bestowed His grace on these believers and saved them. Now they needed to prove their commitment by living out their faith, being obedient to Christ, and becoming mature Christians. His benediction was simple: "Grace be with you all. Amen."

OUTLINE OF THE BOOK OF HEBREWS

I. Christ's Superior Person (1:1—4:16)
  A. Superior Revelation (1:1–14)
    1. The Prophets' Revelation (1:1)
    2. The Present Revelation (1:2a)
    3. The Preeminent Revealer (1:2b–14)
  B. Superior Redemption (2:1–18)
    1. Christ's Stern Warning (2:1–4)
    2. Christ's Sacrificial Work (2:5–18)
  C. Superior Reconciliation (3:1–19)
    1. Explanation of Faithfulness (3:1–6)
    2. Example of Failure (3:7–11)
    3. Exhortation to Faithfulness (3:12–19)
  D. Superior Rest (4:1–16)
    1. Promise of Rest (4:1–3)
    2. Presentation of Rest (4:4–10)
    3. Personal Responsibility (4:11–16)

II. Christ's Sufficient Priesthood (5:1—7:28)
  A. Christ's Priesthood (5:1–14)
    1. The Earthly High Priest (5:1–5)
    2. The Eternal High Priest (5:6–10)
    3. The Exhortation to Hearers (5:11–14)
  B. Christian Perfection (6:1–8)
    1. Progressing in Faith (6:1–3)
    2. Perils of Faith (6:4–6)
    3. Parable on Faith (6:7–8)
  C. Christian's Promise (6:9–20)
    1. The Saint's Position (6:9–12)
    2. The Secure Promise (6:13–18)
    3. The Steadfast Pledge (6:19–20)
  D. Comparison of Christ's Priesthood (7:1–10)
    1. Introduction to Melchizedek (7:1–2)
    2. Identity of Melchizedek (7:3)

E. Consecration of the Saints (10:19–25)
    1. The Christian's Faith (10:22)
    2. The Christian's Faithfulness (10:23)
    3. The Christian's Fellowship (10:24–25)
F. Confronting Church Saints (10:26–39)
    1. Peril of Rejecting the Savior (10:26–31)
    2. Plea to Remember Their Suffering (10:32–34)
    3. Promise of Reward to the Saints (10:35–39)

IV. Christ's Spiritual Priorities (11:1—13:25)
A. Faith of the Saints (11:1–40)
    1. Foundation of Faith (11:1–3)
       a. Essence of Faith (11:1)
       b. Elders of Faith (11:2)
       c. Evidence of Faith (11:3)
    2. Faith before the Flood (11:4–7)
       a. Worshiping by Faith (11:4)
       b. Walking by Faith (11:5–6)
       c. Working by Faith (11:7)
    3. Fathers of Faith (11:8–29)
       a. Submissive Faith (11:8–10)
       b. Sarah's Faith (11:11–12)
       c. Steadfast Faith (11:13–16)
       d. Sacrificing Faith (11:17–19)
       e. Sons of Faith (11:20–22)
       f. Serving by Faith (11:23–29)
    4. Fearless Faith (11:30–31)
       a. Conquering Faith (11:30)
       b. Converting Faith (11:31)
    5. Family of the Faithful (11:32–40)
       a. People of Faith (11:32)
       b. Persecution of the Faithful (11:33–38)

Please note: This outline does not always follow chapter titles and outlines within the chapters.

CHAPTER 1

THE INCOMPARABLE CHRIST
Hebrews 1:1–3

Without question, Hebrews is one of the greatest and most important books in the New Testament. It contains an in-depth study of both the deity and humanity of Jesus the Messiah, covering His earthly ministry to His exaltation at the right hand of God Almighty. This epistle explains the excellence of Christ in His person, priesthood, preeminence, and purpose for coming to Earth.

This epistle was written primarily to Jewish believers, some of whom were thinking about returning to Judaism (Heb. 10:23–25). It encourages them to go on to maturity in Christ (6:1–2) and shows that Christ is better than what Judaism had to offer (1:4; 6:9; 7:7, 19, 22; 8:6; 9:23; 10:34; 11:16, 35, 40; 12:24). By contrast, Hebrews shows that Christ is superior to prophets, angels, Moses, Joshua, Aaron, Melchizedek, the Tabernacle, sacrifices, priesthood, and the Old Testament saints. In other words, the Old Testament prophecies of the Messiah were fulfilled in Jesus (cf. Lk. 24:27, 44).

Even today, the book of Hebrews reminds Jewish believers that Christ is superior to anything they had in Judaism and that He is sufficient for every area of their spiritual lives. The first three verses provide irrefutable proof that Jesus Christ is God and heir of all things.

The Prophets' Revelation

The writer of the epistle wasted no time in making his point. Without any salutation, he immediately began setting forth the progression of

God's revelation through the prophets: "God, who at various times and in various ways spoke in time past to the fathers by the prophets" (Heb. 1:1).

All we know about God came directly from Him. If God had not spoken, humanity would have no clue as to His person, nature, character, or will for mankind. Nor would people know the truth about creation. Thus, over time, God progressively revealed Himself through the prophets who accurately recorded the revelation, revealing God and His will for humanity.

God did not set aside the prophets' personalities, languages, or cultures when He providentially guided each to reveal His Word. All Scripture is God-breathed, infallible, inerrant, plenary, verbal, and confluent as originally given. As the very Word of God, Scripture possesses the properties of authority, sufficiency, clarity, and efficacy.

The revelation from God came at "various times and in various ways" to "the fathers" (v. 1). From the time of Adam to the prophet Malachi, God progressively revealed His plan, program, and purposes. He also spoke in "various ways" to the fathers (v. 1). Often God gave the revelation directly to men, such as Abraham, Moses, Isaiah, and Ezekiel. God also spoke to the prophets through dreams and visions. At other times He spoke through a storm, fire, or an audible voice.

The Old Testament was inerrant truth from God, but it is not all the truth God was to reveal to man. What was revealed in the Old Testament set the stage for unveiling the sufficiency and superiority of Jesus Christ, God's Son. Four hundred years after the close of the Hebrew Scriptures, God would continue His revelation to mankind through Jesus Christ.

The Present Revelation

The revelation to the Hebrew prophets was partial and periodic; the preeminent revelation was to come through Jesus Christ, who would not only speak *for* God but *as* God. The writer of Hebrews said succinctly that God "has in these last days spoken to us by His Son" (v. 2).

The phrase *these last days* (literally, "in the last of these days") means the time in which God will terminate His revelation to man. The phrase was a common rabbinical reference denoting a Messianic period. When Jesus the Messiah came into the world, God—through Him—fully expressed the revelation of Himself and His Word to mankind. In other words, in the last days, the Messianic promises God gave the fathers in the Old Testament came to completion and fulfillment in and through Jesus the Messiah.

In the past, God spoke to mankind through the prophets; but now, in these Messianic times, God speaks exclusively "by Son." (In the Greek, the word *His* is missing.) The absence of an article before the word *Son* speaks of the Son's character and nature. In the past, God revealed Himself through prophets who were mere men; but Jesus the "Son" of God possesses the nature of deity and is the one through whom God is speaking in "these last days."

The prophets spoke the Word of God, but the Son is both the Word of God and God (Jn. 1:1). Thus it is Jesus the Son who expresses the New Testament revelation of all that the Father is and wants revealed to mankind. The apostle John well said, "No one has seen God at any time. The only begotten Son [literally, "God"], who is in the bosom of the Father, He has declared Him" (v. 18).

God the Son, who is deity and equal with God the Father, has intimate fellowship with the Father because He is of the same nature as the Father. It is Jesus who has "declared [explains or exegetes] Him." In other words, Jesus interprets and explains the works and the will of God the Father.

The Preeminent Revealer

The writer then set forth seven reasons why Jesus qualifies to be the final communicator of divine revelation and is infinitely superior to the prophets of old:

(1) *He is Heir.* God the Father "has appointed" Jesus Christ "heir

of all things" (v. 2). It is only natural that He should become the Heir if He is the Son. Behind heirship is the authority to be Lord over all the Father possesses (cf. Ps. 2:7–8). The "all things" include everything in the universe, both now and for eternity. Christ must be God in order to rule forever over the universe.

(2) *He is Creator.* It was through Christ that "He [God] made the worlds [ages]" (Heb. 1:2). The Son of God is presented as the mediating agency in creation, not as a mere instrument or passive tool, but a cooperating agent. The apostle Paul wrote, "For by Him all things were created. . . . All things were created through Him and for Him" (Col. 1:16). This means that all the laws, plans, programs, and purposes that guide and govern the created universe through the "ages" reside in Christ—whether they were unfolded in the past or will be unfolded in the future. The times and ages began with Christ and will culminate in Him (Rev. 22:13).

(3) *He radiates God's Glory.* Christ is the "brightness of His [God's] glory" (Heb. 1:3). The word *brightness* means "radiance" or "effulgence," referring to a light shining or flashing from a luminous source. God the Son is the outshining of the divine glory and majesty of the triune God. Jesus does not simply *reflect* God's glory; He *possesses* it. This fact is best seen at the Mount of Transfiguration when Jesus' glory was unveiled to His disciples: "His face shone like the sun, and His clothes became as white as the light" (Mt. 17:2).

(4) *He represents God.* Christ is the "express image of His [God's] person" (Heb. 1:3). The phrase *express image* means "impression" or "stamp." It refers to an engraved character or impression produced by a die or seal that makes an exact reproduction. Paul wrote, "He is the image of the invisible God" (Col. 1:15). Therefore, Christ is the *exact imprint* of God the Father in His essence, attributes, and character. By studying the Son, we are able to understand the invisible Father.

(5) *He is Sustainer.* Christ is "upholding all things by the word of His power" (Heb. 1:3). The Lord made all things and will inherit

all things. He not only sustains the world but also moves all things that have been created toward the goal that was established for them. In other words, the world's coherence is maintained by Christ who holds all things together and moves them in their proper relationship to one another by "the word [spoken word] of His power" (cf. Col. 1:17).

(6) *He is Redeemer.* Christ is the one who "by Himself purged our sins" (Heb. 1:3). This one who created the world, sustains the world, and will inherit the world also redeemed the world. All Jesus needed to do to create the universe was to speak it into existence. But to "purge our sins," He had to go to the cross and die as our Redeemer and sin-bearer. The Son's ministry to provide purification from sin is one of the major themes of this epistle. The work of redemption was accomplished totally by Christ, who gave Himself as a sacrifice for the purification of sin.

(7) *He is Ruler.* Christ is positioned at God's right hand. Once He finished His work on the cross, He "sat down at the right hand of the Majesty [God the Father] on high" (v. 3). This verse speaks of far more than the Son's finished work of revealing God and redeeming mankind. It speaks of Christ being enthroned in a solemn, formal act to a position of honor, dignity, glory, and authority—which He possessed before creation. Being seated at the right hand of God the Father authenticates His coequal status as God.

What a picture of the incomparable Christ! It is self-evident that the Son's person and work supersede and are superior to any revelation given by the prophets or found in Judaism. Each of these seven characteristics confirms the deity of Christ. This epistle was a strong reminder to Jewish believers who, because of persecution, were ready to abandon their new faith and return to Judaism.

Those who deny that Jesus is the divine Messiah are accusing God of being a liar and His Word of being a lie. God has said in His Word that both Jewish people and Gentiles must put faith in the Lord Jesus Christ, who is the only hope for man's redemption.

CHAPTER 2

THE PREEMINENT CHRIST
Hebrews 1:4–14

After completing His earthly ministry, Christ was restored to the dignity and glory He possessed in eternity past, being enthroned at God the Father's right hand as Heir of all creation. Verses 1–3 present Christ as the authoritative Architect and Administrator of the universe, the one who carries the ages He created and all human history to its God-designed end.[1] The remainder of the chapter declares Christ's preeminence, contrasting His superior ministry to that of angels.

Christ's Position

Verse 3 emphasizes the Son's eternal relationship to the Father, whereas verse 4 presents Christ as the exalted Son of God: "Having become so much better than the angels, as He has by inheritance obtained a more excellent name than they" (v. 4).

The word *inheritance* denotes a past-completed fact with present-abiding results, showing that His possession of the inheritance is permanent. Angels are great and powerful; but none has an inheritance like that of Christ, the Son of God. His name, authority, power, and dominion far exceed that of any created angel (Phil. 2:9–11). And Christ's position is greater than the angels' in its identity, incarnation, and inheritance.

The author then used seven quotations from the Old Testament to convey the deity, sovereignty, and authority of Jesus Christ in contrast to angels, who are merely ministering spirits ready to do God's will:

(1) ***Psalm 2:7.*** This first reference presents the Son as Heir: "For to which of the angels did He ever say: 'You are My Son, today I have begotten You'?" (Heb. 1:5).

This Psalm was originally sung at the coronation of a king, such as David or Solomon. The phrase *I have begotten you* does not refer to the Son's origin of existence, eternal generation, or incarnation because there never was a time when the Son did not exist. Although Jesus Christ was always the eternal Son in relationship to God the Father, He was uniquely appointed and was declared at His resurrection to have the positional right to rule as the Son (cf. Acts 13:33–34). This was never said of any angel.

(2) ***Second Samuel 7:14.*** The second reference comes from 2 Samuel, where God presents the Son as the one who fulfills the covenant made with King David: "I will be to Him a Father, and He shall be to Me a Son" (Heb. 1:5). While this text has a primary reference to David's son Solomon, its greater and final fulfillment is in Christ. Solomon's kingdom was not established but divided, whereas Jesus Christ's Kingdom will be established eternally. It is clear that David's greater Son, Jesus Christ, is the one who fulfilled all the Messianic promises of redemption and will fulfill the Millennial Kingdom blessings in the future.

(3) ***Deuteronomy 32:43; Psalm 97:7.*** "But when He again brings the firstborn into the world, He says: 'Let all the angels of God worship Him'" (Heb. 1:6). This reference is from Deuteronomy 32:43 and Psalm 97:7 as quoted in the Septuagint, the ancient Greek translation of the Hebrew text. The word *again* points to a time when all angels will worship Him, demonstrating openly that they are inferior to the Son.

The phrase *but when He again brings the firstborn into the world* refers to Jesus' Second Coming in judgment. The word for "firstborn" was also used by the apostle Paul in Colossians 1:15. It does not imply that Jesus was created by the Father; He has been coequal with the Father from eternity past. Rather, it speaks of Jesus' existence prior to creation and His sovereignty over it. Thus Jesus is higher than the angels because He created them.

Christ's Preeminence

(4) *Psalm 104:4*. "And of the angels He says: 'Who makes His angels spirits and His ministers a flame of fire'" (Heb. 1:7). This quotation shows the place angels have in God's divine administration throughout the universe. Christ is the one who created and commanded the service of angels, and they minister under Him to carry out His will and purposes.

The words *spirits* and *fire* define the nature of these created beings and describe their qualities and activities. The word *spirits* can also be translated "wind." And like the wind, angels are invisible, powerful, and travel quickly.

The phrase *a flame of fire* refers to the angels' brilliant brightness and appearance and implies they implement God's divine judgment.

Even though angels occupy a high place of service in God's economy, their position is still transitory and far inferior to that of Christ. He is superior to angels because they are subject to His authority and will.

(5) *Psalm 45:6–7*. In this quotation the author affirmed the eternality, majesty, authority, and administration of the Son in God's Kingdom. He also celebrated the Son's status of righteousness in keeping with God's holy character:

> *But to the Son He says: "Your throne, O God, is forever and ever; a scepter of righteousness is the scepter of Your kingdom. You have loved righteousness and hated lawlessness; therefore God, Your God, has anointed You with the oil of gladness more than Your companions"* (Heb. 1:8–9).

These verses declare that Christ has a throne, whereas angels only minister around God's throne. The phrase *scepter of righteousness* symbolizes Christ's universal rule on His eternal throne; His reign is motivated by righteousness. Therefore, God has anointed the Lord Jesus and exalted Him above all His "companions." That is, He was anointed with the Holy Spirit for His office of prophet, priest, and king when He entered His ministry.

Through this Old Testament quotation, the author declared five important truths about Jesus the Son: He is addressed as God by the Father; He is given an eternal throne and Kingdom; He reigns in righteousness; He hates lawlessness; and He is above all angels in His nature, character, eternality, majesty, authority, and rule.

Christ's Power

(6) *Psalm 102:25–27.* These verses were used to speak of God the Father in Psalm 102 but are used here to describe Christ's unchangeableness, eternal power, majesty, and glory:

> *You LORD, in the beginning laid the foundation of the earth, and the heavens are the work of Your hands. They will perish, but You remain; and they will all grow old like a garment; like a cloak You will fold them up, and they will be changed. But You are the same, and Your years will not fail* (Heb. 1:10–12).

Christ was "in the beginning" and created the foundations of both heaven and Earth. This means He had to exist before the beginning. Thus Christ, who created all things, is eternal (Col. 1:16); but heaven and Earth are transitory.

Heaven and Earth are compared to an old garment or cloak that one day will be rolled up and discarded. The current heaven will pass away (Rev. 20:11); and the earth, with everything in it, will burn up (2 Pet. 3:10). Both are now deteriorating. All of creation is transitory and locked in a downward spiral of deterioration and eventual death.

Christ, however, is not transitory. He is eternal, immutable (unchangeable), and permanent: "Jesus Christ is the same yesterday, today, and forever" (Heb. 13:8). And in the future He will create a new heaven and Earth that also will be eternal. Therefore, Christ is superior to angels in nature, existence, power, immutability, destiny, and glory.

(7) *Psalm 110:1.* "But to which of the angels has He ever said: 'Sit at My right hand, till I make Your enemies Your footstool'?" (Heb.

1:13). These words were spoken exclusively to Christ the Son, never to angels. No angel was ever promised a seat at the Father's right hand. The Father's enthronement of Jesus Christ declares His acceptance of the Son and the Son's ministry on Earth.

Christ's enthronement at the Father's right hand foreshadows His enthronement on Earth when He will reign and rule on King David's throne during the Millennial Kingdom (Lk. 1:32–33). In the future, all Christ's enemies will be put under His feet:

> *Therefore God also has highly exalted Him and given Him the name which is above every name, that at the name of Jesus every knee should bow, of those in heaven, and of those on earth, and of those under the earth, and that every tongue should confess that Jesus Christ is Lord, to the glory of God the Father* (Phil. 2:9–11).

The Son is destined to rule the universe in the eternal state of the new heaven and Earth, for "He has on His robe and on His thigh a name written: KING OF KINGS AND LORD OF LORDS" (Rev. 19:16). This verse portrays Christ's complete victory over His enemies. Everything will be put under His authority by God the Father (1 Cor. 15:22–28).

Hebrews 1:14 sums up the angels' status and function compared to the Son: "Are they not all ministering spirits sent forth to minister for those who will inherit salvation?" When Christ's work was finished, He sat down. On the other hand, the work of angels is not finished; they are God's servants to minister to the heirs of redemption. Angels minister to believers by protecting them from evil, defending and delivering them from harm, and bestowing divine benefits on them. This truth should be a great encouragement to us during suffering and hardship.

The phrase *who will inherit salvation* has a present and future fulfillment. Although salvation encompasses regeneration in this life, it involves much more and will culminate with the reception of a glorified body.

No other chapter in the Bible presents such a full picture of the deity of Jesus Christ. He is called Son, Lord, and God. He is omnisc++ient, omnipotent, immutable, and eternal. He is Creator, Sustainer, Redeemer, Ruler of the universe, and Heir of all things in heaven and Earth. He is worshiped by angels and all creatures that ever existed. Thus Jesus Christ is preeminent over the prophets and angels in His person and work.

Endnote

[1] J. Dwight Pentecost, *A Faith That Endures* (Grand Rapids, MI: Discovery House Publishers, 1992), 52.

CHAPTER 3

THE SUPERIORITY OF CHRIST
Hebrews 2:1–18

In the midst of showing Christ's superiority to angels, the author of Hebrews paused to apply what he had presented previously. He then warned and exhorted Jewish believers in Jesus—the recipients of this letter—not to neglect the superior revelation of salvation they have received from Christ. Because of opposition and persecution, these Hebrew Christians were dangerously close to renouncing their commitment to the Messiah. But doing so, the author wrote, would bring inescapable discipline from the Lord.

Christ's Stern Warning

Hebrews 2 begins with a stern warning: "Therefore we must give the more earnest heed to the things we have heard, lest we drift away" (v. 1). *Therefore* points back to the preceding revelation of Christ's preeminence as the Son of God. The phrase *drift away* pictures a boat that is loose from its moorings and is floating into unsafe waters. These Jewish believers were exhorted to heed the revelation, or they would "drift away" from their new faith. The author continued to illustrate his point:

> *For if the word spoken through angels proved steadfast, and every transgression and disobedience received a just reward, how shall we escape if we neglect so great a salvation, which at the first began to be spoken by the Lord, and was confirmed to us by those who heard Him, God also bearing witness both with signs and wonders, with various miracles, and gifts of the Holy Spirit, according to His own will?* (vv. 2–4).

Angels delivered the Old Testament Law to Moses, and it was binding on the house of Israel (Acts 7:53; Gal. 3:19). Those who disobeyed Moses' Law suffered judgment. This being the case, how much greater the judgment would be on all who disregarded revelation through Christ.

Those addressed here are a generation of Jewish believers who did not hear Jesus personally. They received Christ through the witness of apostles who performed signs, wonders, and miracles that authenticated and confirmed their messages were from the Lord. To return to Judaism and the Levitical system would indicate indifference to Christ's revelation and their profession of salvation. If God punished indifference to the Law given through angels, He would certainly punish those who were indifferent to the revelation of His Son.

At this point the author returned to his theme of Christ's preeminence over angels. In Hebrews 1, he revealed that Jesus the Son of God is eternal and coequal with God the Father and is now seated at the Father's right hand. So why did the Son leave heaven and become incarnate? The remaining verses of Hebrews 2 answer that question.

Christ's Sacrificial Work

Christ Is Sovereign. Although angels are great and glorious, the Lord "has not put the world to come [the Millennial Kingdom] . . . in subjection to angels" (v. 5). It was always God's plan to give man dominion over His creation (Gen. 1:27–30). God ordained that man should rule over the earth. Knowing this fact, the author asked a rhetorical question, quoting Psalm 8:4: "What is man that You are mindful of him, or the son of man that You take care of him?" (Heb. 2:6). That is, why does God, who created the vast universe, care for an insignificant creature like weak and puny man who appears as less than a speck in God's universe?

Continuing to quote from Psalm 8, the author cited four facets of God's design for humanity:

(1) *Man is distinguished in rank.* "You have made him a little lower than the angels" (Heb. 2:7). Man was created lower physically since he is limited to Earth, but not lower in spiritual rank.

(2) *Man was created with dignity.* "You have crowned him with glory and honor" (v. 7). In his unfallen state, Adam was the federal head of humanity; and in his exalted position over creation, he was crowned or granted glory and honor.

(3) *Man received dominion.* God "set him over the works of [His] hands" (v. 7). In his unfallen state, man was granted authority and responsibility to rule the world (Gen. 1:28). But after the fall, this privilege was removed.

(4) *Man has a destiny:* "You have put all things in subjection under his feet" (Heb. 2:8).

Because of sin, God set aside—but did not terminate—His original design for mankind to rule the world. At Christ's Second Coming, He will establish the Millennial Kingdom and restore—to redeemed man, this time—the right to rule the earth.

A number of scholars do not believe these verses refer to humanity but to Christ because Jesus used the phrase *Son of Man*, referring to Himself in the Gospels. Although Christ will be the one who ultimately rules over all things (1:13), the author of Hebrews probably had mankind in mind up to this point. Psalm 8 refers to mankind, and the author of Hebrews focused on mankind's status in creation in order to emphasize the exaltation of Christ later in this chapter.

A commentator explained: "The author may have been thinking about the double meaning included in the words 'son of man,' showing that Jesus fulfilled the role and destiny originally commissioned to people. What humans could not do, Jesus will do."[1]

Christ Was Submissive. Jesus came to Earth as a man to redeem mankind from its fallen state·and to regain mankind's original destiny: "But we see Jesus, who was made a little lower than the angels, for the suffering of death crowned with glory and honor, that He, by the grace of God, might taste death for everyone" (Heb. 2:9).

The name Jesus, rather than the title Christ, is used to stress both His humanity and humiliating death on the cross. His mission in coming to Earth is declared in verse 9. Although He is the Creator and Lord over all angels, He took on flesh and became a man, becoming a little lower than the angels. His purpose: to die physically in man's place (paying the price and penalty for the sins of all mankind) so that individuals could be redeemed and reconciled with God. Jesus' humiliating death enables God's grace (unmerited love and favor) to be manifested to all who put their faith in Him.

This entire plan was conceived in eternity past by the determined counsel and foreknowledge of God (Acts 4:28). Upon accomplishing His mission, the Lord arose from the dead and ascended back to heaven, where He is seated in exaltation at the Father's right hand and is crowned with glory and honor.

Christ Secured Salvation. What God the Father did through Jesus was "fitting [proper, suitable, and not out of character] . . . in bringing many sons to glory, to make the captain of their salvation perfect [complete, as having attained its goal] through sufferings" (Heb. 2:10). The word *captain* refers to a pioneering prince or leader within a family. Jesus became a man within the family of mankind in order to become the leader of redemption through His death and resurrection.

Christ Sanctifies Saints. To those who have experienced salvation through faith in Jesus Christ, He becomes their Sanctifier—the one putting them on a path to holiness: "For both He who sanctifies and those who are being sanctified are all of one" (v. 11). Believers are united out "of one" source with Jesus in the sanctifying process, and "He is not ashamed to call them brethren" (v. 11).

This union between Christ and His brethren was spoken of in two Old Testament passages: Psalm 22:22 and Isaiah 8:17–18. Those who come to Christ are united with Him and identified as His "brethren"

(Heb. 2:12; cf. Ps. 22:22). While Jesus endured suffering on Earth and eventual death, He put "trust in Him [God]" (Heb. 2:13; cf. Isa. 8:17 [Septuagint]) and was completely dependent on Him, becoming an example for His brethren to follow. All believers are children of God, and God the Father gave them to Christ (Heb. 2:13; cf. Isa. 8:18 [Septuagint]).

Christ Subdued Satan. Another reason Jesus came to Earth was to set man free from bondage to the Devil's power:

> *As the children have partaken of flesh and blood, He Himself likewise shared in the same, that through death He might destroy him who had the power of death, that is, the devil, and release those who through fear of death were all their lifetime subject to bondage* (Heb. 2:14–15).

Through His death and resurrection, Jesus Christ broke death's power and the Devil's power over death. The word *destroy* does not mean the Devil has been annihilated or is inactive. Rather, at the cross, his power was rendered inoperative or ineffective in holding believers in bondage. Believers have been delivered from spiritual death now and will be delivered from physical death at the Rapture. Thus, those who put faith in Christ no longer need fear the sting of dying because death is swallowed up in the victory and deliverance gained through Christ's sacrificial death and resurrection (cf. 1 Cor. 15:54–57).

Christ Sympathizes With Sufferers. Jesus did not come to bring salvation to angels but to people: "For indeed He does not give aid to [take on the nature of] angels, but He does give aid to [takes on] the seed of Abraham" (Heb. 2:16). It is not angels whom He came to save, but the physical and spiritual seed of Abraham. The verbs in this verse are in the present tense, indicating that Christ's help did not stop with providing salvation; it is ongoing to the redeemed.

Christ became incarnate so that "He might be a merciful and faithful High Priest in things pertaining to God" (v. 17). A high priest in Judaism mediated between God and Israel. He offered sacrifices according to the Mosaic Law and interceded for the sins of the Jewish people. Christ was "merciful," or full of compassion and sympathy, which was often lacking in Aaronic priests who were sometimes unfeeling and cruel. He was "faithful," or showed uncompromising fidelity, in His priestly service to God when He made "propitiation for the sins of the people" (v. 17). In short, propitiation is the aspect of Christ's atoning death that satisfied the righteous demands of God's judicial holiness and wrath (provoked by mankind's sin), thereby making it possible for God to show mercy and bestow salvation on all who believe.

In becoming a man, Jesus experienced human temptation, testing, and suffering: "For in that He Himself has suffered, being tempted [tested], He is able to aid those who are tempted" (v. 18). Feeling the full force of Satan's cunning, power, and wrath, Jesus endured greater testing than any man, being tested "in all points . . . as we are, yet without sin" (4:15).

Thus Jesus is "able to aid," or bring immediate help and relief, to those who cry out for His assistance in their times of testing because He understands their human condition and weakness.

Jesus Christ is superior to angels in His person and work, and He is uniquely qualified to satisfy the righteous demands of God. Jesus provided salvation through His death on the cross and is swift to help people in their times of trouble. So, it behooves everyone, especially believers, to heed the warning not to neglect the Lord or the "so great salvation" He has provided.

Endnote

[1] Bruce B. Barton, David Veerman, Linda Taylor, and Philip Comfort, *Hebrews*, Life Application Bible Commentary (Wheaton, IL: Tyndale, 1997), 20–21.

CHAPTER 4

CHRIST IS SUPERIOR TO MOSES
Hebrews 3:1–19

Moses is a dominant figure in Israel's history. Of all the Old Testament leaders, there is none greater. He is described as "the man of God" and "the servant of the LORD" (Dt. 33:1; 34:5). Moses' relationship with God was so intimate that "the LORD spoke to Moses face to face, as a man speaks to his friend" (Ex. 33:11). Some rabbis even believe Moses was greater than the angels because of his unusually close relationship with God. Yet Moses understood the Lord would raise up a prophet from within Israel who would be much greater than he and who would speak God's Word to Israel (Dt. 18:15–18). This prophet is clearly identified in the New Testament as Jesus the Messiah (Jn. 1:45). Hebrews 3 shows how Christ is superior to Moses and sternly warns Jewish believers that if they return to the Jewish religion, they will be in danger of forfeiting God's rest.

Rest here does not mean salvation. No true believer can lose or forfeit his or her salvation. Jesus made it extremely clear that those to whom He gives eternal life will never perish or be snatched from His hand (Jn. 10:28–29). Christ will not lose one soul the Father has given Him (6:37, 39). Scripture teaches that lives of genuine believers are hidden with Christ in God (Col. 3:3). Therefore, by definition, someone who renounces Christ and returns to Judaism (or to any other religion, for that matter) is not a true believer in the Messiah. However, true believers can lose their "rest," meaning the peace, joy, and assurance that come from a life of faith in Jesus.

Explanation of Faithfulness

The author addressed his readers as "holy brethren, partakers [partners] of the heavenly calling" (Heb. 3:1). That is, they were Jewish believers who made "confession" (v. 1) of Jesus Christ as their Savior. The word *confession* means to "say the same thing as another" or to agree with God on what He revealed about Jesus His Son.

Believers are to "consider the Apostle and High Priest of [their] confession, Christ Jesus" (v. 1). The word *consider* means to fix one's eyes and mind attentively on Christ as Apostle and High Priest. Christ is called an Apostle because God the Father sent Him to provide for mankind's salvation. As an Apostle, Christ represents God to man. He is called High Priest because He is the believer's advocate in heaven, representing man to God before His throne. Thus, as God's Son, Christ functions as Reconciler and Mediator before God and man.

Jewish believers highly esteem Moses as the greatest servant in Israel because of his position before God and his faithful leadership over the nation for 40 years. Moses was definitely great, but Christ is superior to Moses and to all things pertaining to Judaism. To prove this truth to Jewish believers, the author compared and contrasted the ministries of Christ and Moses.

First, both Christ and Moses were "appointed" by God the Father and faithfully carried out their ministries (v. 2; cf. Num. 12:7). Moses was appointed to deliver the Israelites from Egypt, give them the Law, and lead them to the Promised Land. But Christ was even more faithful because, unlike Moses, He did not falter or waver, even to His death on the cross.

Second, Moses was a human servant (Heb. 3:5); but Christ is a divine Servant and, as the Son of God, is "worthy of more glory than Moses" (v. 3).

Third, Moses was a "faithful [servant] in all His [God's] house" and should be granted all the honor, respect, and reward due him (v. 2; cf. Num. 12:7–8). But Christ built and oversees the house of Israel in which Moses served, making Christ more honorable: "For this One has been counted worthy of more glory than Moses, inasmuch as He who built the house has more honor than the house" (v. 3).

Both Jesus and God are called the builder of the house (vv. 3–4). Since all things were created through Jesus Christ (1:2), these verses confirm His deity. If Jewish people returned to Judaism, they would be worshiping the house rather than the Creator or Builder, thus turning from the one who is God, namely, Jesus Christ.

Fourth, "Moses indeed was faithful in all His house as a servant, for a testimony of those things which would be spoken afterward" (3:5). Moses not only was faithful in his ministry but also faithfully witnessed and wrote about Christ (cf. Dt. 18:15, 18; cf. Jn. 5:46; Heb. 11:24–27).

Under Moses, *house* referred to the house of Israel. But in this age the reference is to Christ's position over the church: "Christ as a Son over His own house, whose house we are if we hold fast the confidence and the rejoicing of the hope firm to the end" (3:6).

Verse 6 expresses three thoughts:

(1) *Christ is superior to Moses.* Moses is merely a servant; but Christ is the Son of God.

(2) *Within every household, a son is always superior to a servant.* A servant may have authority to oversee the house, but the son rules over the house and everything in it.

(3) *People with faith will remain faithful.* The phrase *if we hold fast the confidence . . . firm to the end* does not refer to how to become a believer or remain a believer. The author simply said that those who possess faith in Christ will remain faithful, thus giving evidence that they are members of Christ's household.

True believers will continue "rejoicing of the hope" in Christ's redemption to the end of their lives. On the other hand, if someone professes faith in Christ but returns to Judaism, that person reveals that he or she is not a true believer in the Messiah.

Example of Failure

In verses 7–11 God, through the Holy Spirit, provides a quote from Psalm 95:7–11 to warn those professing faith in Christ not to repeat the same sin of murmuring and rebelling that their forefathers committed in the wilderness, culminating in their refusal to take the Promised Land (Num. 13—14).

After 400 years in Egyptian captivity, Israel was miraculously delivered. Yet the Israelites continually complained about God and Moses on the way to possess the Promised Land. At one point, the Lord commanded Moses to send two representatives from each of the 12 tribes to search out the land of Canaan.

The spies returned with a mixed report. All agreed Canaan was a good and fruitful land, flowing with milk and honey. Nevertheless, its people were strong and lived in walled cities (Num. 13:27–29). Of the 12 spies, only Joshua and Caleb had faith to believe God would deliver the Canaanites into their hands. Israel's refusal to take the land constituted rebellion against God, resulting in His displeasure and judgment of that generation of Israelites:

> *Therefore, as the Holy Spirit says: "Today, if you will hear His voice, do not harden your hearts as in the rebellion, in the day of trial in the wilderness, where your fathers tested Me, tried Me, and saw My works forty years. Therefore I was angry with that generation, and said, 'They always go astray in their heart, and they have not known My ways.' So I swore in My wrath, 'They shall not enter My rest'"* (Heb. 3:7–11).

The word *today* in verse 7, quoted from Psalm 95:7, is repeated twice more in this chapter (vv. 13, 15) and sends an urgent message to Jewish believers to heed God's Word immediately and not make the same mistake as their forefathers.

Their forefathers disobeyed God in six ways. They (1) failed to "hear His [God's] voice," (2) hardened their hearts, (3) rebelled, (4) tested and tried Him, (5) always went astray in their hearts, and (6) never really knew Him.

In other words, they neglected to listen to, or chose to forget, what God told them through Moses. Failing to listen produced hard hearts (v. 8). Hardness of heart resulted in rebellion against God.

During Israel's 40 years of wandering, it witnessed many miracles but still "tested" and "tried" God by complaining and rebelling (v. 9). Instead of taking Him at His Word, Israel put Him to the test, making Him prove that He could do or would do all He had promised them.

Such distrust was gross sin and angered God. It also was inexcusable, since the Israelites had witnessed God's miracles and provisions for 40 years. So God's evaluation was that they erred habitually: "They always go astray in their heart" (v. 10; cf. Dt. 9:24).

Though the Israelites saw God's mighty miracles, knew what He expected of them, and had His Law to lead them, God said of them, "They have not known My ways" (Heb. 3:10).

Israel's unbelief and rebellion grieved God, and He became justly "angry with that generation" (v. 10). Consequently, Israel would suffer God's wrath, or righteous indignation, as He destroyed that generation in the wilderness. Israel's lack of faith resulted in the nation not entering God's "rest" (v. 11); that is, that generation would not possess and occupy the Promised Land of Canaan.

Exhortation to Faithfulness

In Hebrews, Jewish people are strongly exhorted to avoid the defection of their forefathers who went off into unbelief:

> *Beware, brethren, lest there be in any of you an evil heart of unbelief in departing from the living God; but exhort one another daily, while it is called "Today," lest any of you be hardened through the deceitfulness of sin* (vv. 12–13).

This is a command that believers take heed and keep a watchful eye over their lives. Drawing away from commitment to the Lord can result in apostasy.

The remainder of chapter 3 exposes the process of becoming an apostate. A person departs from God due to "an evil heart of unbelief" (v. 12). An evil heart allows the "deceitfulness of sin" to control the believer. Sin is described as being "deceitful," or tricky, because it subtly seduces those whose spiritual guard is down; and they succumb to Satan's attack. Sin that is not dealt with will produce an unexpected, gradual hardness of heart, making believers indifferent; cold; callus; and insensitive to God and spiritual things (v. 13).

Christians are to "exhort [encourage] one another daily" and stay focused on Christ because they are "partakers [partners] of Christ" (vv. 13–14). The real test of these professing believers is to "hold the beginning of [their] confidence [in Christ] steadfast to the end" (v. 14).

Again the author emphasized the word *today*, alerting Jewish believers that they, too, were in danger of developing the same hardness of heart and rebellious attitude toward God as their forefathers "who came out of Egypt" (vv. 15–16).

Though God was angry with those persistent sinners, He patiently showed them mercy for 40 years; but eventually they perished in the wilderness as punishment for their unbelief (v. 17). This was a direct fulfillment of God's promise to unbelieving Israel. He preserved only Caleb and Joshua because they believed Canaan could be conquered (v. 18; Dt. 1:34–40).

Because of unbelief, these Israelites missed entering the Promised Land and the rest God had prepared for them (Heb. 3:19). "Trials, troubles, temptation, testing, travail, turmoil, and tempest was their lot in place of the tranquility they might have enjoyed" had they believed and obeyed God.[1]

The illustration, instruction, and invitation given in this chapter were not only for Jewish believers in the early church, but for us today. All who harden their hearts against God will forfeit His rest and suffer His discipline. This example sends a sobering message to all who profess faith in Christ. God will discipline believers who harden their hearts and rebel against Him.

Endnote

[1] Herman A. Hoyt, *Christ—God's Final Word to Man* (Winona Lake, IN: BMH Books, 1974), 24.

CHAPTER 5

THE REST GOD GIVES
Hebrews 4:1–13

Chapter 3 of Hebrews presents two types of rest: that of entering Canaan (the rest offered to Israel) and that which comes from a life of faith in Christ. All the Israelites 20 and older, except for Joshua and Caleb, were denied life and rest in the Promised Land of Canaan because they rebelled against God in unbelief after He redeemed them from Egypt (Heb. 3:18–19). Chapter 4 urges readers not to miss the rest God now provides in Christ.

Promise of Rest

The author warned Jewish believers in Jesus who were suffering severe persecution not to succumb to the same fate as their forefathers: "Therefore, since a promise remains of entering His rest, let us fear lest any of you seem to have come short of it" (v. 1).

Some considered returning to Judaism to escape persecution. But by doing so, they would fall "short" of the life of faith and rest that God had designed for them.

What does the author mean by *rest?* Some teach it speaks of the personal salvation that results in eternal life. This is doubtful because those redeemed out of Egypt and those addressed in Hebrews were believers, not unbelievers. No true believer can lose his or her salvation. Scripture clearly teaches that the lives of believers are hidden with Christ in God and that Christ will not lose one soul the Father has given Him (Jn. 6:37, 39; Col. 3:3).

Others teach that *rest* refers to the Millennial Kingdom rest at Christ's Second Coming. Although both millennial and eternal rest will be granted to all believers, neither one was the rest promised to the Israelites when they took possession of the Promised Land under Joshua. Theirs involved security, protection, the guarantee of God's presence, and rest from war (Dt. 12:9–11).

The rest promised in Hebrews is appropriated by faith in Christ and produces peace, harmony, and joyful fellowship with Him even amid opposition and conflict in the world.

Jewish believers delivered out of Egypt and those in addressed in Hebrews were given God's message: "For indeed the gospel was preached to us as well as to them; but the word which they heard did not profit them, not being mixed with faith in those who heard it" (Heb. 4:2).

The "gospel" proclaimed in Moses' day was the good news of divine grace bestowed on Israel. It was good news that Israel was delivered from Egyptian bondage, given a sacrificial system that covered sins through blood atonement, and given the Promised Land. The gospel Jewish believers heard in Hebrews was that of salvation through Jesus Christ.

Both groups received God's Word, but it did not profit those under Moses because it was not mixed with faith. Many Israelites rebelled in unbelief, desiring to return to Egypt. Hebrews warns Jewish people professing faith in Christ not to make the same error, for the gospel is of no profit unless it is believed and received by faith.

"For we who have believed do [now] enter that rest, as He has said: 'So I swore in My wrath, "They shall not enter My rest,"' although the works were finished from the foundation of the world" (v. 3). In other words, today God's rest is only obtainable through faith in Christ. Through Jesus, people can receive "the peace of God, which surpasses all understanding" (Phil. 4:7). Those who rebelled under Moses did not receive God's promised rest because they died in the wilderness due to their unbelief.

Presentation of Rest

God's rest for both Israel and believers in Christ was "finished" in eternity past, before God created the world.

> *For He has spoken in a certain place of the seventh day in this way: "And God rested on the seventh day from all His works"; and again in this place: "They shall not enter My rest." Since therefore it remains that some must enter it, and those to whom it was first preached did not enter because of disobedience* (Heb. 4:4–6).

God rested on the seventh day (Gen. 2:2), signifying that He was satisfied with His creation; nothing more was needed. This does not mean God became inactive, but rather, His purpose and plans for creation and humankind were completed.

The author boldly repeated his warning using Psalm 95 (cf. Heb. 3:10–11, 18–19; 4:3), driving home the seriousness of missing out on God's rest because of disobedience. Although Israel failed to enter God's rest, that rest remained available for future generations of believers. The author proved his point by using two Old Testament illustrations.

The rest offered to Israel in the wilderness was reoffered in David's day: "Again He designates a certain day, saying in David, 'Today,' after such a long time, as it has been said: 'Today, if you will hear His voice, do not harden your hearts'" (Heb. 4:7; cf. Ps. 95:7–8, 11; Heb. 3:7–8, 15).

Since no permanent rest for Israel was established in Moses' day, it was reoffered to David's generation. But David's generation failed to trust in God as well. Therefore, the permanent rest God offered in David's day would be reoffered to the Jewish people and to all who received Christ through faith. Again, the author strongly warned his readers not to turn from the Lord in hardness of heart but to put faith in Christ quickly lest they suffer the same fate as their forefathers.

Nor did the Israelites find rest in Joshua's day:

For if Joshua had given them rest, then He [God] would not afterward have spoken of another day. There remains therefore a rest [literally, "Sabbath rest"] for the people of God. For he who has entered His rest has himself also ceased from his works as God did from His (Heb. 4:8–10).

In other words, if Joshua had given Israel a complete and final rest when the new generation entered the Promised Land, then God would not have reoffered rest to Israel under David 500 years later, as recorded in Psalm 95. Since Israel under Moses, Joshua, and David did not appropriate the rest offered, there still remains a rest for the "people of God."

The Greek word for "rest" (*sabbatismos*) in Hebrews 4:9 differs from the word (*katapauo*) used elsewhere in chapters 3 and 4 and from the physical rest of Canaan that Israel anticipated enjoying. *Sabbatismos* refers to the rest God enjoyed after creating the universe (4:4) and pronouncing with satisfaction that it was "good."

Furthermore, this rest does not involve keeping the Sabbath as practiced in Judaism. Neither is it acquired by works. Rather, this promise of rest is the joyful fellowship, peace, and harmony that believers experience now through faith in Christ and the solace they will enjoy when life's pains and struggles are ended and they enter the eternal rest promised by God (Rev. 14:13).

Personal Responsibility

The author then challenged and exhorted readers to take personal responsibility and act on what he said: "Let us therefore be diligent to enter that rest, lest anyone fall according to the same example of disobedience" (Heb. 4:11).

The author concluded his argument by urging professing Jews not to return to Judaism because God's Word will detect whether their faith in Christ is real. One might deceive himself and others, but not God.

He also made five statements in verse 12 concerning how God's Word works in the life of a professing believer:

(1) *"The word of God is living."* Since revelation is God-breathed, it is alive and therefore able to give spiritual life to those who are spiritually dead.

(2) *It is "powerful."* The word of God actively works in believers to teach them doctrine, diagnose sin, discipline them, and provide direction for them when they hear and heed it.

(3) *It is "sharper than any two-edged sword."* Like the short Roman sword of the day, sharp on two sides, it can deeply penetrate an individual, cutting in every direction (Eph. 6:17).

(4) *It is "piercing even to the division of soul and spirit, and of joints and marrow."* As a knife divides flesh from bone, God's Word penetrates the soul and spirit, revealing what is deep inside an individual.

(5) *It is "a discerner of the thoughts and intents of the heart."* The word *discerner* (Greek, *kritikos*) means "critic" or "judge" and speaks of one who has the capability and right to judge. God's Word strips away the façade; delves deep into a person's heart; and exposes his or her true thoughts, motives, attitudes, and intentions—good and evil.

Therefore, "there is no creature hidden from His sight, but all things are naked and open to the eyes of Him to whom we must give account" (v. 13). God knows (sees) everything in His creation, no matter how small or secretive. The deeds, thoughts, imaginations, and intentions of our hearts and souls are exposed to God for what they are, because God's Word exposes them.

The word *open* pictures a wrestler bending back the neck of his opponent in a death grip—leaving him prostrate, powerless, defenseless, and defeated. Likewise, every heart is "open," or powerless, defenseless, and defeated before God and His Word.

This is a graphic warning concerning one's commitment and accountability before God. And it admonishes all people to make their salvation sure by accepting Jesus' invitation, "Come to Me . . . and you will find rest for your souls" (Mt. 11:28–29).

CHAPTER 6

THE GREATEST HIGH PRIEST
Hebrews 4:14–16

The importance of the high priesthood of Jesus Christ cannot be overstated. Christ's high priesthood is mentioned briefly in Hebrews 2:17 and 3:1; but the subject is fully developed in Hebrews 4:14—10:25 and forms a major theological theme in the book of Hebrews, more so than in any other New Testament book.

Although verses 4:14–16 are brief, they should not be skimmed over because they present an important snapshot of what follows:

(1) Christ is the believer's great High Priest.

(2) Believers should hold tenaciously to their professions of faith in Christ.

(3) Believers should be greatly encouraged because, through Jesus Christ, God has made a way they can go with bold confidence directly to the throne of grace and ask for help.

First the author showed that Christ is superior to the prophets, angels, Moses, and Joshua. Next he proved that Christ's high priesthood is superior even to that of Aaron.

Christ's Priesthood

Addressing Jewish people considering a return to Judaism, the Scripture immediately establishes that Jesus Christ is the believer's High Priest: "Seeing then that we have a great High Priest who has passed through the heavens, Jesus the Son of God, let us hold fast our confession" (v. 14).

The concept of a priesthood did not originate with the nation of Israel. During the patriarchal period, the head of each household functioned as a mediating priest on behalf of his family members, offering sacrifices to God on their behalf (Gen. 12:7–8; 13:18; 22:9; Job 1:5).

At Mount Sinai, God informed Israel that if the nation obeyed Him, it would become "a kingdom of priests and a holy nation" (Ex. 19:6). The Israelites would have direct access to Him, along with the responsibility to demonstrate His holiness to the world.

But the Israelites sinned against God and broke the covenant He had made with them at Mount Sinai, forfeiting the privilege of becoming a Kingdom of priests (v. 5). Therefore, it became necessary for God to choose priests from among the people to represent the nation of Israel before Him.

While Moses was on Mount Sinai, God said to him, "Now take Aaron your brother, and his sons with him, from among the children of Israel, that he may minister to Me as priest" (28:1). Thus God chose the tribe of Levi to function as priests (Num. 3:5–13). The term *priest* (Hebrew, *kohayn*) means "one who officiates." The high priest in Judaism was not an angel and did not possess supernatural qualities; he was a mere man with the same nature and passions of any other man.

In comparison, Jesus' priesthood is entirely different. Jesus is identified as a "great" High Priest because He is the divine Son of God (Heb. 1:1–4; 3:6). For Jesus to be a High Priest, He had to take on the seed of Abraham and become a man like His brethren (2:16–17), yet without sin. He was sent into the world by appointment through the authority of God the Father (Jn. 17:18; 20:21); and after His death, resurrection, and ascension, He superseded the Aaronic priests.

Our great High Priest is not on Earth today but has "passed through the heavens" (Heb. 4:14). After His crucifixion, resurrection, and 40-day postresurrection ministry, Jesus ascended through the atmospheric and stellar heavens into the third heaven, to be seated in exaltation at God the Father's right hand (1:3). There He intercedes for believers as an Advocate with God the Father.

The author exhorts Jewish believers, along with all believers, "Seeing then that we have a great High Priest who has passed through the heavens, Jesus the Son of God, let us hold fast our confession" and not waver in commitment to Him (4:14). Early Jewish believers would demonstrate their confession and possession of Jesus were genuine by sticking with the faith amid severe opposition and persecution.

Today Jesus is the only High Priest Jews and Gentiles alike have to represent them before God. His shed blood on the cross efficaciously atoned for the sins of mankind, and He is the only Mediator between God and man. By faith in Him and His finished sacrifice on the cross, any person can have his or her sins forgiven.

Christ's Perfection

Although Christ returned to heaven to occupy His rightful position at the Father's right hand, He is still very much aware of our plight and needs: "For we do not have a High Priest who cannot sympathize with our weaknesses, but was in all points tempted as we are, yet without sin" (v. 15).

During His earthly pilgrimage, Jesus Christ was fully aware of the problems that plague mankind. As He increased in wisdom and stature and grew in favor with God and man, He was tempted as we are. He became tired, hungry, and thirsty and experienced human limitations. He felt pain, love, rejection, joy, sorrow, peace, and fear. He endured poverty and persecution and was forsaken by His friends when He needed them most; even God the Father deserted Him on the cross.

Satan pursued Him throughout His life and with subtle cunning attempted to entice Him to sin. The Devil did all in his power to destroy Christ during His earthly ministry. No better words sum up His suffering than those of the prophet Isaiah:

He is despised and rejected by men, a Man of sorrows and acquainted with grief. And we hid, as it were, our faces from Him; He was despised, and we did not esteem Him (Isa. 53:3).

The types of temptations Jesus faced are recorded in Matthew 4:1–11. The Holy Spirit led Jesus into the wilderness to be tested by the Devil. At His weakest moment, after He had fasted 40 days, Jesus was approached by the Devil, who used the same ploy he used against Eve in the Garden of Eden: He appealed to the lust of the flesh, lust of the eyes, and the pride of life (Gen. 3:6; cf. 1 Jn. 2:16). Satan's entire purpose was to cause the Son of God to sin and, in so doing, destroy Him and His ministry.

First, the Devil appealed to the flesh, tempting the Lord to satisfy His physical desire for food by turning stones into bread (Mt. 4:3).

Second, the Devil appealed to pride, tempting the Lord to prove His deity by jumping from the Temple's pinnacle, whereupon His angels would swoop down and miraculously preserve Him from injury (vv. 5–6).

Third, the Devil appealed to the eyes, tempting the Lord with power and dominion. He took Jesus to a high mountain and showed Him the kingdoms of this world and their glory, promising to give all of them to Him in return for worship (vv. 8–9). If Jesus had succumbed, He would have made Himself subservient to an inferior, created being and moved totally outside of God's will.

In all three temptations, Jesus did not argue with the Devil or resist him in His own power. He overcame the temptations by accurately quoting passages from Deuteronomy.

Jesus was "in all points tempted as we are, yet without sin" (Heb. 4:15). The word *yet* is not in the original Greek text. So the passage should read "without sin," that is, "apart from sin." In other words, sin was not a temptation to Him because there was nothing in Him to respond to sin.

The fact that Jesus did not sin is confirmed by Scripture: He "knew no sin" (2 Cor. 5:21), "committed no sin" (1 Pet. 2:22), and was "apart from sin" (Heb. 9:28). Sin was not inherent in Him because He did not possess the Adamic nature. The Lord could be tempted because He was human; but as the God-Man, it was impossible for Him to sin. If God can sin, then He is not God. The same holds true for the Son of God.

Some people ask, "Since Jesus was sinless and it was impossible for Him to sin, was His temptation real?" Yes, it was very real because it came to Him from outside His being. However, He could not, and did not, yield to it. For example, a man in a small boat might attack a battleship and try to sink it with a bow and arrow. The attack and intent are real, but it is impossible for arrows to sink a battleship.

Having been tested by temptation, Jesus was touched with the feeling of our infirmities; He knows, understands, and sympathizes with the human condition. We now have a Man in glory as our High Priest who triumphed over temptation and functions as our Mediator, Intercessor, and Advocate.

Christ's Provision

Knowing that Christ is their High Priest in heaven who completely understands their plight and persecution, Jewish believers are encouraged to take advantage of Jesus' availability. The author closed this section with a call to prayer and a reminder of the Lord's provisions: "Let us therefore come boldly to the throne of grace, that we may obtain mercy and find grace to help in time of need" (4:16).

Under the Mosaic Covenant, Israelites were unable to go before God's throne. They obtained access through the high priest who was only allowed into God's presence once a year, on the Day of Atonement. And he entered with fear and trembling. In contrast, Jewish believers are continually bidden to come into God's presence with boldness, confidence, frankness, and free and open speech to pour out their hearts at the throne of grace. Notice that believers come to a throne of grace, not a throne of judgment.

They receive mercy when they confess their past sins, and mercy to help them face their current miseries. Grace is how God dealt with believers in the past when they received Christ. Grace also provides God's enablement to meet their needs. Believers undergoing persecution today can take great solace, hope, and encouragement in the Lord.

No matter what the need, whether it be for forgiveness, wisdom, self-control to overcome a sinful habit, strength in one's walk with the Lord, food, clothing, or any insufficiency, you can make your plea at God's throne of grace. The admonition is to go boldly, and you will receive abundantly.

What a High Priest! What glorious promises! What a privilege for believers! God's throne of grace is open to all who avail themselves of it.

CHAPTER 7

CHRIST IS SUPERIOR TO AARON
Hebrews 5:1–14

The tribes of Israel revered the Aaronic high priest. With the exception of Moses, he enjoyed greater access to and fellowship with God than any other Israelite. Although God bestowed him with privilege, position, and prominence, he nevertheless was imperfect and subject to infirmities and death—like any other man.

By contrast, Christ's priesthood is superior. He is the perfect and eternal High Priest whose sacrifice and ministry remain, to this day, more excellent than Aaron's. Hebrews 5:1—10:25 describes His ministry.

The Earthly High Priest

The author of Hebrews began by reviewing the qualifications and essential ministry of the Aaronic high priest. First, he was in solidarity with man: "For every high priest taken from among men is appointed for men in things pertaining to God" (5:1). To qualify for the position, the high priest had to be mortal, from the seed of Abraham and the tribe of Levi. His sole function was to represent men to God and God to men.

Second, he was neither self-appointed nor elected but, rather, divinely selected: "No man takes this honor to himself, but he who is called by God, just as Aaron was" (v. 4).

Some, like Korah, Dathan, and Abiram, arrogantly challenged Aaron's divine appointment as high priest, claiming he assumed too much authority as Israel's sole representative before God (Num. 16:1–3). So Moses brought Korah and his followers before the Lord with censers of incense and fire to determine whom the Lord had ordained. God overwhelmingly confirmed Aaron's high-priestly call when He made the ground open and swallow Korah and all who had rebelled with him (vv. 1–32). Aaron's rod then miraculously budded, proving further that he was God's choice (chap. 17).

Third, the high priest also was to sympathize with men so that he could "have compassion on those who are ignorant and going astray, since he himself is also subject to weakness" (Heb. 5:2). Like his brethren, he possessed physical weaknesses, experienced temptation, sinned, and would one day die and give an account for his works before God. Being conscious of his limitations made him compassionate for (literally, "deal gently with") the people he served.

His ministry involved offering sacrifices for his sins and those of the people (vv. 1, 3). There were five specific sacrificial offerings and five animals, along with incense, that the priest was to offer daily and on various feast days, in accordance with the Hebrew calendar. (See Leviticus 1—7.) On the Day of Atonement, the high priest alone was allowed to offer incense and blood sacrifices in the Holy of Holies for the sins of Israel (Lev. 16).

The Eternal High Priest

For Christ to qualify as High Priest, He needed to be human, divinely appointed, compassionate, and able to offer Himself as a sacrifice for sin. Jesus met all these qualifications. But, unlike Aaron, He is an eternal High Priest.

The author confirmed Christ's qualifications by quoting from two Messianic psalms: Psalms 2 and 110. Using Psalm 2:7 he showed that, as the eternal Son of God, Christ was appointed High Priest by God the Father: "So also Christ did not glorify Himself to become High Priest, but it was He [God the Father] who said to Him: 'You are My

Son, today I have begotten You'" (Heb. 5:5). The phrase *I have begotten You* does not refer to the Son's origin, eternal generation, or incarnation because there never was a time when He did not exist. Rather, the author verified that, at Christ's resurrection, Jesus was uniquely appointed as High Priest and declared to be so by God the Father. The same was never said of Aaron.

Christ's priesthood is from a different order than was Aaron's. Quoting Psalm 110, he called Christ "a priest forever according to the order of Melchizedek" (v. 6, cf. Ps. 110:4). Melchizedek was a king-priest; Aaron was only a priest. No Israelite king dared enter the Temple to function as a priest without experiencing God's severe judgment (cf. 2 Chr. 26:16–21). Like Melchizedek, Christ is both a King and Priest.

The Aaronic high priesthood was inherited and transmitted to many sons throughout the centuries. Melchizedek, however, stood alone. Like Jesus, he neither inherited his kingly priesthood nor transmitted it to successors.

Typifying the eternality of Christ, Melchizedek had no recorded ending, though Aaron had to be replaced upon his own death. Furthermore, the Aaronic priesthood ceased with the destruction of Herod's Temple in A.D. 70.

To be a high priest, Christ needed to be human. So He took on flesh and became a man. The phrase *in the days of His flesh* (Heb. 5:7) refers to Christ's entire earthly pilgrimage as a mortal until He was resurrected and glorified (cf. 2:14, 17).

As a man, the Lord "offered up prayers and supplications, with vehement cries and tears to Him who was able to save Him from death, and was heard because of His godly fear" (5:7). This reference must be to the Lord's agony in the Garden of Gethsemane the night before He was crucified. It was there His soul was overcome with sorrow as He grieved in prayer over what He soon would face.

From which death was Christ praying to be delivered? He could not have longed for escape from death in general because He was born into the world for that purpose. He could not have feared death by crucifixion because He predicted He would die in this manner (Mt. 20:19). Nor could He have feared premature death in Gethsemane where Satan tried to destroy Him to prevent Him from becoming a sacrifice for sin. Christ had absolute control over His own death (Jn. 10:18). He was not praying to be resurrected from the grave because He predicted His resurrection while ministering on Earth (Mt. 16:21; 20:19).

Christ knew He must become a sin offering for humankind. Through His death, He satisfied the righteous demands of a holy God, making it possible for Him to provide salvation and forgiveness of sin to all who believe.

Christ prayed in the garden, "If it is possible, let this cup pass from Me; nevertheless, not as I will, but as You will" (Mt. 26:39). What Christ feared was the excruciating agony of eternal separation from God the Father whose presence He had enjoyed since eternity past. The Father heard the Son's "godly fear [reverence]" and granted His petition (Heb. 5:7). Although Jesus experienced spiritual separation from the Father during His death on the cross, He was eternally reunited with God the Father after His resurrection.

Christ is a sympathetic High Priest because He suffered in His humanity: "Though He was a Son, yet He learned obedience by the things which He suffered" (v. 8). To feel as others do, Christ had to experience life on a human level (Lk. 2:52). He faced all the trials and temptations that other men do; but unlike other men, He was completely obedient to God the Father (cf. Mt. 4:1–11). In fact, He said, "I always do those things that please Him [the Father]" (Jn. 8:29).

Christ also provided salvation through the sacrifice of Himself: "And having been perfected, He became the author of eternal salvation to all who obey Him" (Heb. 5:9). Of course, He was not morally incomplete. But through His sacrificial death on the cross, He completed, or brought to fulfillment, the work of salvation designed in eternity past. He is the "author" (literally, "principal cause") of our "eternal salvation." Salvation is not bestowed universally on everyone; it is given only to those who put their faith in Him.

Through His suffering, obedience, and sacrifice, Christ is fit to be "called [designated or greeted] by God as High Priest 'according to the order of Melchizedek'" (v. 10). Like Melchizedek, Christ is a "priest forever" (v. 6). Unlike the Aaronic priesthood, His ministry is permanent because He continually intervenes on behalf of believers.

The Exhortation to Hearers

The author had much more to say about Christ's high priesthood (v. 11) but was reluctant to do so for three reasons: his readers' spiritual condition, spiritual capacity, and spiritual callousness.

First, they were "dull [slothful] of hearing" (v. 11). They had drifted from and become insensitive to the deeper teaching regarding Christ's priesthood.

Second, they were infantile in their faith:

> *For though by this time you ought to be teachers, you need someone to teach you again the first principles of the oracles of God; and you have come to need milk and not solid food* (v. 12).

Although they had been believers for some time, they had not grown because they were lazy in their spiritual lives.

Unable to digest the solid meat of God's Word, they needed to be taught the elementary truths of the faith. Such people are "unskilled in the word of righteousness," for they are babes (v. 13). Babes in Christ lack the cognitive skills to perceive or rationally receive and understand God's Word. Though beautiful to behold at first, they become spiritually grotesque if they remain babes for years.

Third, lazy believers are callous when it comes to discerning "good and evil" (v. 14). Mature Christians who study and apply both the elementary and profound truths of God's Word possess the spiritual insight needed to "discern both good and evil" (v. 14). However, those who fail to apply what they have learned remain spiritual babes forever. To glorify Jesus Christ our High Priest, we must grow in the knowledge of God's Word and strive toward spiritual maturity.

CHAPTER 8

MATURING IN CHRIST
Hebrews 6:1–8

Maturing in Christ is a process; it doesn't happen overnight. Unfortunately, some people never get there. They regress rather than progress. Hebrews 6 warns believers in Jesus to forsake practices that hinder their spiritual growth and urges them to advance to full maturity in Christ.

Speaking to Jewish believers in particular, the author first unfolded Christ's glorious priesthood. Then he abruptly changed the subject to address the callousness of believers who had become slothful in their spiritual growth (5:11–14). Rather than mature in their faith, they were in danger of returning to the Levitical system from which they had been delivered.

Progressing in Faith

The author listed the elementary principles these believers needed to move past:

> *Therefore, leaving [putting away, not repudiating] the discussion of the elementary principles [literally, "beginnings"] of Christ, let us go on to perfection, not laying again the foundation of repentance from dead works and of faith toward God, of the doctrine of baptisms, of laying on of hands, of resurrection of the dead, and of eternal judgment. And this we will do if God permits* (6:1–3).

Scholars disagree on whether these items are Christian teachings, elements of Judaism that these new believers still practiced, or both. Six "elementary principles" appear in three sets of two each:

(1) **Conversion.** The first pair of principles addresses conversion: "not laying again the foundation of [1] repentance from dead works and of [2] faith toward God" (v. 1). At the time of their salvation, these people evidenced repentance from dead works and faith toward God. Repentance is only acceptable to God the Father when one turns from his or her old life and embraces Jesus Christ for the forgiveness of sin. In fact, the Levitical system never provided salvation (cf. Heb. 10:1–4, 10). It provided an awareness of sin. Salvation has always been through faith. Since Christ's death and resurrection, true "faith toward God" is experienced only through receiving Jesus Christ.

(2) **Ceremonial Cleansing.** The second set of principles addresses ceremonial cleansing: "the doctrine [teaching] of [1] baptisms [washings], of [2] laying on of hands" (v. 2). Because the word *baptisms* is plural, it could refer to the Levitical system's ceremonial rites of cleansing. Judaism incorporated many ceremonial washings, both in worship and daily living. Jewish believers probably carried some of these practices into their Christian experience, and now they needed to put them away.

"Laying on of hands" may refer to a practice connected with presenting an offering in the Temple. An Israelite typically placed his hands on the sacrificial animal's head as a symbol of identification. A twofold identification took place: The Israelite's sinful life was committed to the animal, and the offering's acceptability was transmitted to the Israelite (Lev. 1:4; 3:8, 13). New believers may have continued offering Levitical sacrifices in Temple worship.

This phrase may also refer to the early church's practice of laying on of hands during believer's water baptism. The laying on of hands was used as a symbolic act of identification, authentication, and confirmation of the apostles' ministry when the Holy Spirit was initially poured out in the early church (Acts 8:17); it is not to be regarded as a "second blessing."

(3) *Coming Events.* The third set of principles addresses "resurrection of the dead" and "eternal judgment" (v. 2). These doctrines were first taught to new believers at the time of their salvation, and their importance cannot be overstated. Before their redemption, Jewish people believed in a resurrection from the dead (Job 19:23–27; Dan. 12:1–3), but their understanding was extremely limited. In the apostles' preaching, the resurrection finds full meaning in Jesus Christ who is "the resurrection and the life" (Jn. 11:25). Although understanding the resurrection is extremely important, believers must mature beyond this basic teaching.

Jewish people also believed in eternal judgment as taught in the Old Testament, but their knowledge on this subject also was fragmented and limited. They learned a great deal more about eternal judgment as revealed through Jesus Christ, and they needed to embrace this more thorough teaching.

Confident that his readers would progress to maturity, the author wrote, "And this we will do if God permits" (v. 3). The phrase *if God permits* does not ask if it is God's will to mature in Christ but, rather, assumes it is His will.

Perils in Faith

The author then issued one of the strongest warnings in the New Testament:

> For it is impossible for those who were once enlightened, and have tasted the heavenly gift, and have become partakers of the Holy Spirit, and have tasted the good word of God and the powers of the age to come, if they fall away, to renew them again to repentance, since they crucify again for themselves the Son of God, and put Him to an open shame (vv. 4–6).

This passage has been misunderstood, misinterpreted, and misapplied; and it rates among one of the most controversial texts in the New Testament. The most predominate interpretations are these: (1)

These people lose their salvation. (2) These are professing believers who never possessed salvation. (3) This is a hypothetical situation that could never happen. (4) Those who received enlightenment about salvation, tasted the heavenly gift, and became partakers of the Holy Spirit never received Jesus Christ as Savior. (5) These are saved people who lost their rewards. (6) These are saved people being exhorted to mature in Christ. This last interpretation best fits the context of Hebrews 5:11—6:8.

The author reviewed five spiritual truths that believers experience when coming to the Lord. First, they "were once [once-for-all] enlightened" (6:4). At the time of their salvation, these people were spiritually permeated with the light of the gospel and clearly perceived, understood, and appropriated it for their salvation.

Second, they "tasted the heavenly gift." The word *taste* means more than to sample something; it speaks of full participation. The author used *taste* to refer to Christ's death (2:9). Christ did not merely sample death; He experienced it. Throughout the New Testament, the word *gift* is used to refer to the blessings associated with salvation and eternal life. These are saved people who received the gift of eternal life when they received Christ.

Third, they "have become partakers of the Holy Spirit." The word *partakers* means to share or participate in something. The author used this word concerning the Incarnation of Jesus Christ who partook of "flesh and blood" at His physical birth (2:14). Consequently, these people were not simply associated with the Holy Spirit; they were actually indwelled with the Holy Spirit at the moment of salvation.

Fourth, they "have tasted the good word of God" (6:5). That is, they heard and received the spoken Word that they knew came from God.

Fifth, they tasted or experienced "the powers [miracles] of the age to come." They were eye witnesses to the miracles Christ and the apostles performed (2:4), and they believed those miracles were from God. Christ will manifest these same powers more fully in the "age to come," meaning in the Millennial Kingdom.

The evidence indicates that those mentioned here are not merely professors but possessors of salvation. Wrote Dr. J. Dwight Pentecost: "All the words the writer uses—*enlightenment, tasted, become partakers*—are never used in the New Testament of empty profession, but always of an actual experience. Thus there can be no question that the apostle viewed the recipients as believers."[1]

Speaking of people who were redeemed but might later decide to return to Judaism, the author wrote, "For it is impossible . . . if they fall away [deviate, turn aside, or wander from the true faith], to renew them again to repentance, since they crucify again for themselves the Son of God, and put Him to an open shame" (6:4, 6).

What does verse 6 mean? First, verse 4 says it is "impossible" for believers to do what is mentioned in verse 6.

Second, the phrase *fall away* is an aorist participle in Greek and refers to a point when one might abandon his faith, but no specific reference to an actual abandonment is given. The words *fall away* cannot mean a loss of salvation because it is not possible to lose one's salvation; and if it were possible, the text would mean such individuals could never again become saved.

Third, the word *if* in the phrase *if they fall away* is absent from the Greek text; the verse should read "and then have fallen away." Thus, the verse contains no hint of a conditional element. Fourth, should a person return to Judaism, "it is impossible" (v. 4) to "renew [restore] them again to repentance" (v. 6).

In other words, those who willfully defect from Christianity after receiving its great spiritual privileges could never be brought back to repentance. Why? Because "to their loss [with respect to themselves] they are crucifying the Son of God all over again and subjecting him to public disgrace" (v. 6, NIV).

Such attitudes and actions amount to a public rejection of Christ and an affirmation before His enemies, who condemned and crucified Him, that His death was deserved. To renew such people to repentance (not conversion but recommitment) would be almost impossible because of their extreme hardness of heart. If such people remained so indifferent after being chastening by the Lord, they would be at a point of no return and would remain perpetually in a state of spiritual immaturity.

Parable on Faith

The author used an agricultural analogy to further clarify his argument:

> *For the earth which drinks in the rain that often comes upon it, and bears herbs useful for those by whom it is cultivated, receives blessing from God; but if it bears thorns and briers, it is rejected and near to being cursed, whose end is to be burned* (vv. 7–8).

Rain here is compared to God's provision for creation and is symbolic of His spiritual blessings on all believers. Believers are compared to a field upon which the rain falls. The field that is properly sowed and tilled receives rain and produces fruit.

Another field receives rain but produces only thorns and briers. What the unfruitful field produces is "rejected," meaning disapproved (cf. 1 Cor. 9:27). It is "cursed" and its produce is gathered to be "burned" (Heb. 6:8). The field itself, however, will survive. In other words, the person's works will be burned at the Judgment Seat of Christ (1 Cor. 3:11–15; 2 Cor. 5:10), but the individual will not (cf. 1 Cor. 3:15; Jn. 15:6). Anyone who refuses to grow spiritually or returns to a system of good works will be disapproved, resulting in the loss of reward.

This warning is to all believers today. Those who have become dull of hearing, callous, or stagnant in their faith must leave spiritual infancy behind and move on toward maturity in Christ.

Endnote

[1] J. Dwight Pentecost, *A Faith That Endures* (Grand Rapids, MI: Kregel, 1992), 104.

CHAPTER 9

A SURE HOPE
Hebrews 6:9–20

In the previous eight verses of this chapter, the author encouraged new believers to leave the traditions of Judaism and press on toward maturity in Christ. Failure to do so, he warned, would disastrously affect their spiritual lives. However, he was confident that such would not be the case for a true child of God; thus his warning is offset by an encouraging, positive message.

The Saint's Position

The author expressed confidence in the steadfast commitment of these believers: "But beloved, we are confident of better things concerning you, yes, things that accompany salvation, though we speak in this manner" (Heb. 6:9). The word *beloved* sets the tone of this hope-filled message and underlines the author's affection for these Christians. *Beloved* is never used to address unsaved people or apostates.

Furthermore, he was "confident [persuaded] of better things concerning [them]." Earlier he had misgivings about their commitment, but now he was convinced they would press on from infancy to maturity in Christ.

God had already witnessed the fruit of their salvation, and He "is not unjust [unfair] to forget" what they have done (v. 10). Verse 10 lists what God will not forget: (1) their "work and labor of love" to the point of exhausting themselves in the Lord's service; (2) that the purpose of their service was to bring praise and glory "toward His [God's] name";

and (3) that they did so by faithfully ministering "to the saints." God would not forget their unselfish service helping others, because He is righteous and fair in rewarding every good deed.

The author again appealed to these believers, encouraging them to continue in their commitment to the Lord: "And [But] we desire that each one of you show the same diligence [earnestness] to the full assurance of hope until the end, that you do not become sluggish, but imitate those who through faith and patience inherit the promises" (vv. 11–12).

This is the same appeal originally made in Hebrews 5:11–14. By showing earnestness in quickly taking to heart the truth they were previously given in Christ, they demonstrated "full assurance" of the salvation hope they possessed. Without being fully persuaded of one's salvation, an individual lacks stability in his or her walk before the Lord and will not progress toward maturity in Christ. Without settled convictions, people are tossed about by various doctrinal teachings and will eventually fall in their commitment to Him.

Consequently, believers must not "become sluggish" in the faith but must show spiritual diligence by becoming grounded in the truth of God's Word (v. 12). In so doing, they will possess the hope, or assurance, of salvation; and that hope will carry them "until the end," or to the day their spiritual pilgrimage on Earth has reached its goal.

Another way to guard against spiritual sluggishness is to "imitate those who through faith and patience inherit the promises" (v. 12). The word *imitate* means to "mimic, model, or emulate" men and women of faith who were approved by God in Scripture. In chapter 11 the author listed people whose faith these believers should emulate. The classic example is the apostle Paul who said, "Imitate me, just as I also imitate Christ" (1 Cor. 11:1). These believers were expected to exercise "faith and patience [endurance]," like those in Hebrews 11, until they inherited the promises that would be theirs in the Kingdom Age.

The Secure Promise

The epistle then uses Abraham as proof that God's promises are immutable:

> *For when God made a promise to Abraham, because He could swear by no one greater, He swore by Himself, saying, "Surely blessing I will bless you, and multiplying I will multiply you." And so, after he had patiently endured, he obtained the promise* (vv. 13–15).

The writer chose Abraham for many reasons:

(1) Jewish believers could easily relate to him because they had a vital relationship to him in Judaism.

(2) Abraham's greatness and frequent appearance in Scripture made him a good example.

(3) He is considered the father of faith (Gal. 3:16).

(4) God's promises to Abraham were extremely detailed and can be traced through the Bible.

(5) God promised and delivered spiritual blessing to the world through Abraham.

(6) Abraham is an example of someone who exercised faith and endurance, as he waited many years for God to fulfill His promises.

(7) God swore by Himself because He could swear by no one greater, confirming that He would fulfill His promises made to Abraham (Heb. 6:13).

When making an oath, a person always vows by a greater power than himself to assure the fulfillment of his oath. In this situation, God condescended to employ the custom of the day. He swore by the greatest authority in the universe—Himself—putting His own integrity, reputation, and honor on the line to guarantee the fulfillment of His promises to Abraham.

Proving his point, the author said, "Surely blessing I will bless you, and multiplying I will multiply you" (v. 14). This is a quote from

Genesis 22:17 where God promised to bless Abraham by multiplying his seed. The fulfillment did not come immediately: "And so, after he had patiently endured, he obtained the promise" (Heb. 6:15). Abraham had to be content to rest in God's promise until God chose the proper time to fulfill it.

In fact, Abraham was 75 when he received the promise (Gen. 12:4), and Isaac was not born until 25 years later (21:5). It would be another 60 years before his first grandchild would be born (25:26), 15 years before Abraham's death (v. 7). Yet Abraham was content to endure patiently until "he obtained the promise." Hebrews teaches believers to emulate his faith. Since God kept His promises to Abraham, He will assuredly keep the promises made in Jesus Christ to those who put their trust in Him.

Disputes in biblical times were often settled by an oath:

> *For men indeed swear by the greater, and an oath for confirmation is for them an end of all dispute. Thus God, determining to show more abundantly to the heirs of promise the immutability of His counsel, confirmed it by an oath, that by two immutable things, in which it is impossible for God to lie, we might have strong consolation, who have fled for refuge to lay hold of the hope set before us* (Heb. 6:16–18).

This passage stresses the importance of an oath. Over the centuries, the veracity of a person's testimony in a court of law has been validated using oaths. In years gone by, in an American court of law, a person about to testify was requested to place his left hand on a Bible, lift his right hand, and swear to tell "the truth, the whole truth, and nothing but the truth, so help me God." The individual was swearing by an authority higher than himself, and the highest authority is God. The individual was guaranteeing the truthfulness of his testimony and invoking God as his witness.

God had no need to make an oath. His say-so would have been

sufficient. But He went a step further and "confirmed it by an oath" (v. 17). He thus condescended to mankind's level to prove without any doubt that He will unconditionally and without reservation fulfill His promises to Abraham. His oath stresses the volition of His will and the "immutability of His counsel" (v. 17). Here God is both the giver and guarantor of the promise He made not only to Abraham but also the "heirs" (v. 17) of Abraham's physical seed. Since God's counsel is immutable, His promises will be fulfilled.

God swore the oath based on "two immutable things": the promise and pledge (v. 18). First are the unconditional, immutable promises He gave Abraham in Genesis 12:1–4 and 15:1–6. Second is God's confirmation of the pledge when He vowed to fulfill the oath made to Abraham by a covenant in Genesis 15:7–21. The promise and pledge are immutable because fulfillment is based totally on God's character. They are fully trustworthy because they are based on the truthfulness of God's eternal Word, and "it is impossible for God to lie" (Heb. 6:18).

These facts provided not only a "strong consolation [encouragement]" to Abraham but to all believers "who have fled for refuge to lay hold of the hope set before [them]" (v. 18). The phrase *fled for refuge* refers to one of the six Israelite cities of refuge where people could flee for protection if they accidentally killed someone (Num. 35). In like manner, believers may flee, or "lay hold of," refuge in Jesus Christ for salvation and protection, which is their "hope."

In God's Word, hope is never a wish but a settled confidence and conviction possessed by those who rest in the promise of salvation granted by God. In context, this hope is the settled confidence each believer may acquire through spiritual maturity in Christ.

The Steadfast Pledge

The author abruptly changed his figure of speech from a city of refuge to an anchor. Jesus is the believer's "anchor of the soul, both sure and steadfast, and which enters the Presence behind the veil, where the forerunner has entered for us, even Jesus, having become High Priest forever according to the order of Melchizedek" (Heb. 6:19–20).

An anchor secures a ship from drifting. Believers are securely anchored in Christ. And though life's storms beat against him, they can never destroy a believer's position before God in heaven. His soul is securely anchored in God's inner sanctuary, the safest location in the universe. Jesus has entered "behind the veil" into the inner sanctuary of God's presence in heaven. Christ tore the veil away through His death on the cross, making it possible for us who believe to come boldly into God's presence (4:16).

Christ is not only our "forerunner" in heaven, but our High Priest as well (6:20). He inaugurated (opened for the first time) a "new [newly slain] and living [life-giving] way" for people to come with "boldness" (confidence) into God's presence (10:19–20). Through Christ, a believer's hope is safely and securely anchored in heaven.

Thus the author concluded his argument on maturity by returning to the major theme of chapter 5: that Jesus is a "High Priest forever according to the order of Melchizedek" (6:20).

CHAPTER 10

WHO IS MELCHIZEDEK?
Hebrews 7:1–10

First-century Jewish believers faced some perplexing questions concerning Christ's high priestly ministry. Why wasn't He called a priest while here on Earth? How could He be a legitimate high priest and how could His atoning work be efficacious if He was not from the tribe of Levi?

The writer to the Hebrews reached back into the Old Testament and, under inspiration of the Holy Spirit, presented an obscure truth that had been hidden for two millennia. Christ is High Priest after the order of Melchizedek. Melchizedek is mentioned earlier (5:6, 10; 6:20); but chapter 7 makes a fuller comparison, revealing that the Melchizedekian order was superior to the Aaronic one.

Much controversy has revolved around Melchizedek, who is one of the most significant types in Scripture to validate Christ's high priestly ministry. He stepped briefly onto the stage of biblical history and then vanished; little is known of his background.

Introduction to Melchizedek

Melchizedek is first mentioned in relation to Abraham. After Abraham and his nephew Lot parted, Lot eventually moved to Sodom. Later four kings from the East invaded and defeated a coalition of five kings in the Jordan Valley. On hearing that the Eastern kings had abducted Lot from Sodom, Abraham marshaled 318 militarily trained men from his household and, in a nighttime assault, rescued his nephew, along with the spoils the invaders plundered from Sodom and Gomorrah. While returning from the war, Abraham was met by Melchizedek, the king of Salem and priest of God Most High, who brought out bread and wine (Gen. 14:1–18).

In Abraham's presence, Melchizedek offered two blessings. First, he said, "Blessed be Abram of God Most High" (v. 19; cf. Heb. 7:1). He recognized that Abraham had victory because he put faith and trust in God to provide it. Abraham did not receive, nor would he accept, any honor from the king of Sodom; but he did accept honor from Melchizedek.

Second, the king of Salem blessed God: "And blessed be God Most High, who has delivered your enemies into your hand" (Gen. 14:20). Melchizedek honored God for Abraham's miraculous victory. Although Abraham exercised great faith in waging war against the four kings, it was the Most High God who deserved the glory and honor in providing success.

Abraham responded by giving Melchizedek "a tithe [one-tenth] of all" of the spoil (v. 20; cf. Heb. 7:2). (Notice, tithing began with Abraham at least 400 years before the Law of Moses was given.) Abraham's response demonstrates three points: the victory belonged to God; the spoils of war rightfully belonged to God; and a portion of the spoils should be dedicated to honor God.

Identity of Melchizedek

The book of Hebrews identifies Melchizedek in one long sentence:

> *For this Melchizedek, king of Salem, priest of the Most High God, who met Abraham returning from the slaughter of the kings and blessed him, to whom also Abraham gave a tenth part of all, first being translated "king of righteousness," and then also king of Salem, meaning "king of peace," without father, without mother, without genealogy, having neither beginning of days nor end of life, but made like the Son of God, remains a priest continually* (7:1–3).

These verses reveal a number of facts about this individual:

(1) **Melchizedek's name means "king"** (from the Hebrew, *melech*) of "righteousness" (Hebrew, *tzedek*). Thus he was a king who ruled in righteousness—a type of Christ who, in His person and ministry, established true righteousness.

(2) **Melchizedek was the king of Salem** (later identified as Jerusalem), which means "peace" (Ps. 76:2). Righteousness and peace characterized Melchizedek's rule. After His Second Coming, Christ will reign in righteousness; and Jerusalem will become the city of peace.

(3) **Melchizedek was a "priest of the Most High God** [Hebrew, *El Elyon*]," which means "God the Highest," speaking of the true and living God. The God of Israel established Melchizedek's priesthood, yet it was not of the same order as the Aaronic priesthood that God later established.

(4) **Melchizedek was "without father, without mother, without genealogy** [descent]." There is no record of his predecessors or successors. Since Melchizedek was a man, he had both a father and mother; but unlike Aaron's lineage, nothing is recorded in Scripture about his descent, birth, or when he was appointed by God to become a king-priest. Israel placed great importance on a priest's genealogy. Priests had to be able to prove they were qualified to function within the Levitical system. But no genealogy appears for Melchizedek.

(5) **Melchizedek had neither "beginning of days nor end of life."** There is no record of his birth or death because he "remains a priest continually." In comparison, the Levitical priesthood began and ended at a specific point in history. Thus Melchizedek's priesthood is like Christ's in its timelessness.

(6) **Melchizedek's priesthood was like Christ's** in its unlimited scope, while the Levitical priesthood ministered only to Israel.

(7) **Melchizedek was "made like the Son of God"** (Heb. 7:3).

Some say this verse implies a theophany, or preincarnate appearance of Christ, similar to His appearance to Abraham (Gen. 18:1). However, the text simply states Melchizedek was made *like* the Son of God (v. 3), not that he *was* the son of God.

Dr. Homer A. Kent, Jr. provided four compelling reasons why Melchizedek was not the preincarnate Christ:

> *(1) Melchizedek is said to be "made like the Son of God." This is strange language if the sense is that he was actually the Son of God. To argue on the basis of a pagan king's statement regarding the fourth figure in the fiery furnace, "one like a son of the gods" (Dan. 3:25 ASV), is hardly convincing. (2) The statement of Psalm 110:4 calls Messiah a priest "after the order of Melchizedek." This clearly differentiates Christ and Melchizedek, and it would hardly be a clarification if the text said he was a priest after the order of himself. (3) The historical record indicates that Melchizedek was king of a city-state in Canaan, a situation involving a fairly permanent residence on the part of the king. This would be totally without precedent so far as Old Testament revelation regarding theophanies is concerned. These were always temporary manifestations. (4) To argue from etymology that Melchizedek ("king of righteousness") was a theophany has its hazards. Historical and archaeological data indicate good reason to understand compounds with -zedek as reflecting a dynastic title for Jebusite kings of the areas. We have the Biblical example of Adonizedek, king of Jerusalem, in Joshua 10:1 (whose name is even more impressive); yet it can hardly be suggested that this wicked king was a theophany.*[1]

In other words, he was not an angel, superhuman individual, or the preincarnate Christ. He was merely a man who was a king and is continually a priest. No other person in Scripture is identified as a king-priest apart from Melchizedek and Jesus Christ.

Importance of Melchizedek

To convince the Hebrew Christians of Melchizedek's great importance, the author explained the king's superiority to Aaron using two illustrations from the Old Testament.

First he asked readers to consider Abraham's and Aaron's responses to Melchizedek's greatness: "Now consider how great this man was, to whom even the patriarch Abraham gave a tenth of the spoils" (Heb. 7:4).

Abraham was in a position of superiority as patriarch and progenitor of the nation of Israel. But even with his pedigree, he realized Melchizedek was superior to him. And though he was under no obligation to tithe to Melchizedek, he voluntarily abased himself and generously gave the king-priest a tenth of the spoil taken from the four kings he defeated (vv. 2, 4; cf. Gen. 14:20).

Second, he discussed the Levitical priesthood that came through Aaron:

> *And indeed those who are of the sons of Levi, who receive the priesthood, have a commandment to receive tithes from the people according to the law, that is, from their brethren, though they have come from the loins of Abraham; but he whose genealogy is not derived from them received tithes from Abraham and blessed him who had the promises. Now beyond all contradiction the lesser is blessed by the better. Here mortal men receive tithes, but there he receives them, of whom it is witnessed that he lives* (Heb 7: 5–8).

In the Law of Moses, God ordained that Levitical priests were to receive tithes from the Israelites, putting them in a superior position to those who gave the tithes. Melchizedek was not a Levite because Levi, Abraham's great grandson, had not yet been born. Melchizedek and Abraham were contemporaries.

Furthermore, Melchizedek never demanded that Abraham give him the tithe; Abraham gave it voluntarily. Melchizedek accepted it and then blessed Abraham (Gen. 14:19–20). The Greek word for "blessed" in Hebrews 7:6 is in the perfect tense, indicating the result of Melchizedek's historical action has lasting significance. His blessing was more than mere praise for paying tithes; it was an expression of approval from God. Melchizedek is indisputably greater than Abraham. It then follows that, if Melchizedek is greater than Abraham, he is also greater than the Levites who descended from Abraham. Therefore, Melchizedek's priesthood is superior to the Levitical priesthood.

In addition, the Levitical priests died, but Melchizedek's death is never mentioned. This does not mean Melchizedek never died but, rather, that Scripture is silent concerning his death. Thus, in type, his priesthood is eternal—another reason Melchizedek's priesthood is superior to Aaron's and the Levites'.

The author concluded this section on the importance of Melchizedek by saying, "Even Levi, who receives tithes, paid tithes through Abraham, so to speak, for he was still in the loins of his father when Melchizedek met him" (vv. 9–10).

In other words, the Levitical priests, although yet unborn, paid tithes to Melchizedek through their ancestor Abraham—the lesser (Levi) paying tithes to the greater (Melchizedek).

The beautiful truth presented in this chapter shows the greatness of the Lord Jesus' high priesthood. Melchizedek, the king-priest, was superior to Aaron, Israel's high priest. But with all his greatness, Melchizedek was only a type of the true High Priest, Jesus Christ, who is preeminent over all priests. Thus Christ is the Priest who can meet the needs of all believers everywhere, Jewish and Gentile.

Endnote

[1] Homer A. Kent, Jr., *The Epistle to the Hebrews* (1972; reprint, Winona Lake, IN: BMH Books, 2002), 127.

CHAPTER 11

CHRIST'S PERFECT PRIESTHOOD
Hebrews 7:11–28

Many first-century Hebrew Christians struggled to understand the priesthood of Jesus Christ. Growing up under the Levitical system of animal sacrifices, they had centered their faith in the Aaronic priesthood and Mosaic Law. Hebrews 7:11–28 shows why the Levitical priesthood had to be replaced for theological reasons and, in great detail, explains that Christ's priesthood is superior.

Christ's Priesthood Is Perfect

The Levitical system could not bring people to "perfection" (completeness or maturity):

> *If perfection were through the Levitical priesthood (for under it the people received the law), what further need was there that another priest should rise according to the order of Melchizedek, and not be called according to the order of Aaron? For the priesthood being changed, of necessity there is also a change of the law* (Heb. 7:11–12).

The Law was transitory, and it was abrogated at Christ's resurrection. Christ was a Priest, not after the order of Aaron, but after the order of Melchizedek.

Since the priesthood was changed, "of necessity there is also a change of the law" in connection with the priesthood. The Law, being "holy and just and good" (Rom. 7:12), demanded perfect righteousness— something that sinful men who functioned as priests could never provide. Therefore, mankind's hope for perfect standing before God had to be brought about outside the Aaronic priesthood and Mosaic Law. Thus Christ is the only one qualified to function as High Priest on behalf of sinners. This was a new concept in the first century, and many Jewish people found it difficult to understand and accept; their faith had been centered in the Aaronic priesthood and Mosaic Law for centuries. Yet Jesus' own words in Mark 2:21–22 state that their new faith could not be poured into old wineskins or used as a patch to strengthen their Jewish beliefs.

Christ's Priesthood Is Permanent

Hebrews 7:13–19 provides a number of reasons why Christ's perfect priesthood supersedes Aaron's.

First, Christ was not from the tribe of Levi but from "another tribe, from' which no man has officiated at the altar" (v. 13). Christ sprang from Judah, from King David's seed (Isa. 11:1; Mt. 1:1; Acts 2:29–31; Rom. 1:3), "of which tribe Moses spoke nothing concerning priesthood" (Heb. 7:14). Although this concept was new to first-century Jewish believers, God graciously planned and foretold this development centuries before it occurred. Christ would be a different type of Priest, one in the "likeness of Melchizedek" (v. 15).

Second, the Aaronic priesthood was "according to the law of a fleshly commandment" (v. 16). The Levitical priesthood had to be done away with because it sprang out of the Mosaic Law. The Law stipulated that only the family of Aaron from the tribe of Levi could function in the priesthood (Num. 18:1–32). If Christ were to be a Priest, He would need to be from a different order.

Unlike the Aaronic priesthood, Christ's priesthood was "according to the power of an endless [indissoluble] life" (Heb. 7:16). He is the eternal Son of God (Jn. 1:1); Creator and Sustainer of all things (Col. 1:16–17); and, unlike an Aaronic priest, has power to bestow eternal life (Jn. 11:25–26). Whereas the Aaronic priesthood eventually ceased, Christ's appointment as High Priest will last forever because He is "a priest forever according to the order of Melchizedek" (Heb. 7:17; cf. Ps. 110:4).

Third, for the Aaronic priesthood to change, it was necessary to change the Law (Heb. 7:12). There needed to be the "annulling [putting away or making void] of the former commandment because of its weakness and unprofitableness [uselessness]" (v. 18). The Law was unprofitable because (1) it was unable to make people perfect, that is, to complete the process by producing eternal life; (2) it was not possible for the blood of animal sacrifices offered by the Aaronic priesthood to take away sins (10:4, 11); and (3) it was also impossible for the Law to provide or produce righteousness.

Consequently, "the law made nothing perfect [complete]" (7:19). It was incapable of bringing people into a right standing before God. In fact, the Law never brought people near to God; it kept them far from Him. The apostle Paul called the Law "our tutor to bring us to Christ, that we might be justified by faith" (Gal. 3:24). The Law was added because of sin "till the Seed [Christ] should come" (v. 19), enabling people to be justified by faith in Christ as the *only* way to be declared righteous before God (v. 23).

However, the Law did pave the way for a "better hope" (Heb. 7:19) through the new priesthood of Christ, who could bring people to a perfect (complete) standing before God. In other words, it was necessary that the Law and Levitical priesthood be put away for Christ to function as a perfect High Priest. The new priesthood of Christ opened a way of access "through which we draw near to God" (v. 19). Through Christ, all believers are encouraged to come boldly to God's throne of grace to obtain mercy and find grace to help in time of need (4:14–16).

Fourth, Christ's priesthood is sealed with an eternal oath by God; the Aaronic priesthood was not:

> *And inasmuch as He was not made priest without an oath (for they have become priests without an oath, but He [Christ] with an oath*

by Him [God the Father] who said to Him [Christ]: "The L<small>ORD</small> has sworn and will not relent [change His mind], 'You are a priest forever according to the order of Melchizedek'"), by so much more Jesus has become a surety of a better covenant (7:20–22).

A key difference between these two priesthoods is that Christ's is sealed with an eternal oath insuring its perpetual validity, and the Levitical priesthood was not. Thus Christ was made a Priest by an eternal oath providing "a surety," or guarantee, that He will fulfill the promises made in the "better covenant" (New Covenant) that God inaugurated through His shed blood.

Fifth, Christ's priesthood is superior to the Aaronic priesthood in that it is not interrupted by death. The Aaronic priesthood was temporary; its priests would die and be replaced (v. 23). In contrast, Christ's priesthood will never be terminated "because He continues forever, [and] has an unchangeable priesthood" (v. 24). Unlike the Aaronic priesthood, Christ's priesthood is incapable of being altered, passed on to a successor, or terminated—because He is eternal and His priesthood will abide forever.

Consequently, Christ "is also able to save to the uttermost those who come to God through Him" (v. 25). The word *uttermost* speaks of the comprehensiveness or completeness of our salvation. Christ saves the total person (body, soul, and spirit) from the power and penalty of sin, and at our glorification He will deliver us from the presence of sin.

Christ is able to provide such complete salvation because "He always lives to make intercession" for us (v. 25). The word *intercession* encompasses Christ's entire ministry on behalf of believers, based on the merits of His sacrifice. He is an ever-living Priest who continually intercedes for the needs of all believers before God's throne in heaven.

Christ's Priesthood Portrayed

After describing the perfection and permanence of Christ's high priesthood, the author culminated his argument by exhorting, "For such a High Priest was fitting for us" (v. 26). In other words, because of His character, Christ is the only High Priest suitable to officiate before God on behalf of sinful mankind. In simplistic beauty, the writer now pulls together the salient features of what he presented, painting a final portrait of Christ's great priesthood.

His Person. Christ is "holy, harmless, undefiled, separate from sinners, and has become higher than the heavens" (v. 26). *Holy* (Greek, *hosios*) speaks of the innate purity of Christ's character. He is "harmless" (guileless) or free from malice and deceit of any kind. He is "undefiled," free from any moral impurity. He is "separate from sinners"; though He ate and drank with sinners, Christ never sinned. He "has become higher than the heavens." Christ has entered into God's presence, being enthroned in the highest place of honor and power. His character makes Him a fitting High Priest to meet humanity's needs.

His Provision. Christ "does not need daily, as those high priests, to offer up sacrifices, first for His own sins and then for the people's, for this He did once for all when He offered up Himself" (v. 27). Aaronic priests *continually* had to offer sacrifices for themselves and others because the blood of bulls and goats could not take away sin (Heb. 10:4). In contrast, Christ did not have to offer a sacrifice for His own sins, for He is sinless. Yet for the sins of mankind He offered Himself, once for all, as a blood sacrifice to expiate sins. His sacrifice makes Him a fitting High Priest to meet all the needs of mankind.

His Perpetual Priesthood. "For the law appoints as high priests men who have weakness, but the word of the oath, which came after the law, appoints the Son who has been perfected forever" (7:28).

To persuade Jewish believers of Christ's sovereign priesthood, the writer pulled together the threads of all he had previously stated, contrasting the two priesthoods. Aaronic priests were ordained under the Law, but Christ's perfect priesthood is since the Law (cf. Ps. 110:4), showing that He superseded them. Aaronic priests were ordained by the

Law, but Christ was ordained by "the word of the oath, which came after the law" (Heb. 7:28). The Aaronic priests had infirmities (weakness of the flesh), but Christ is perfect. They served only during their lifetimes, but Jesus Christ the Son is a Priest forever. Christ's consecration as High Priest is perfect and permanent in every detail and will continue eternally.

With great enthusiasm, the author exhorted, "We have such a High Priest, who is seated at the right hand of the throne of the Majesty in the heavens" (Heb. 8:1).

Jesus is an unchangeable High Priest who offered Himself as a sacrifice for sin once for all. He is an ever-living Priest whom we will someday see face to face and enjoy throughout eternity, a Priest who is able to save to the uttermost and is seated at God's right hand, making intercession on our behalf. With the apostle Peter we exclaim, "Lord, to whom shall we go? You have the words of eternal life" (Jn. 6:68).

CHAPTER 12

CHRIST'S NEW COVENANT MINISTRY
Hebrews 8:1–13

Hebrews 8 begins with the author summing up the first seven chapters about Christ's priesthood: "Now this is the main point of the things we are saying: We have such a High Priest, who is seated at the right hand of the throne of the Majesty in the heavens" (v. 1). The chapter then shows that the Aaronic priesthood in the Levitical system was superseded by Christ's heavenly priesthood—not through the Mosaic Covenant but through a New Covenant. The author hoped that clarifying these facts would deter Jewish believers from returning to the old Mosaic system that was terminated with Christ's crucifixion.

New Covenant Priest

This section of Scripture presents three reasons why Christ's priesthood is more excellent than the Levitical one:

Majesty. After His resurrection, Christ sat down at the right hand of God the Father. He did not sit on David's throne in heaven, as some teach, because Christ will sit on that throne (in Jerusalem) after His Second Coming (Lk. 1:32–33). The word *seated* (Heb. 8:1) shows that, unlike Levitical priests, Christ completed His work of redemption and has been elevated in heaven to a position of acceptance, authority, power, and honor. Thus Christ is more excellent because of His position of majesty.

Ministry. He is also "a Minister of the sanctuary and of the true tabernacle which the Lord erected, and not man" (v. 2). The words *true tabernacle* point out that the heavenly sanctuary where Christ now operates was erected by God and differs in nature from the Old Testament Tabernacle and Temple erected by people on Earth.

The Levitical high priest was "appointed to offer both gifts and sacrifices" (v. 3). As an appointed High Priest, Christ must offer gifts and sacrifices to God the Father on behalf of those He represents. The Law disqualified Christ from ministering in the Aaronic priesthood on Earth because He was not a Levite (v. 4). Thus He began His high priestly ministry in the heavenly sanctuary after His resurrection.

From their inception, the earthly Tabernacle and its ministry were merely the "copy and shadow of the heavenly things" (v. 5). Since they were only temporary, patterned after heavenly realities, they needed to give way to Christ's superior ministry in heaven.

Mediation. Third, Christ is the "Mediator of a better covenant, which was established on better promises" (v. 6). A mediator is someone who brings two individuals together to consummate an agreement. Moses was the mediator of the covenant given at Mount Sinai (Gal. 3:19); Christ is the Mediator of the New Covenant (Heb. 9:15). The Mosaic Covenant's promises were conditional, earthly, temporary, and applied only to those under the Law. The New Covenant is unconditional, spiritual, and eternal. Christ's death and shed blood on the cross paid the price necessary to implement the New Covenant (cf. Mt. 26:28), providing forgiveness of sin and salvation to all who believe in Him.

New Covenant Priority

The first covenant (Mosaic Covenant) is then contrasted with the second (New Covenant): "For if that first covenant had been faultless, then no place would have been sought for a second" (Heb. 8:7).

The first covenant was made with the nation of Israel at Mount Sinai

(Ex. 19:5; 34:27–28). It did not alter, annul, or abrogate the provisions of the Abrahamic Covenant because the Mosaic Covenant was given 430 years after the Abrahamic (Gal. 3:17–19). Moses carefully distinguished between these two (Dt. 5:2–3).

The Mosaic Covenant encompassed three areas of Israel's life: the moral laws, spelled out in the Ten Commandments (Ex. 20:1–17); the social laws, given to govern relationships within the nation (21:1—24:11); and the religious laws, provided to direct the Israelites in their worship of God (Ex. 24:12—31:18).

But the Mosaic promises of blessing were conditional. Israel had to obey the commandments for God to fulfill His promises: "If you will indeed obey My voice and keep My covenant, then you shall be a special treasure to Me above all people" (19:5).

Israel failed to keep its part of the bargain. The fault was not with the Law, for its commandments were holy, just, and good (Rom. 7:12). Nor was the fault with God, for He directed and led the Israelites out of Egypt with signs and wonders and cared for them throughout their wilderness journey (Dt. 1:30–31; 32:1–14). The fault was with mankind's sinful nature, which caused Israel to rebel against the Mosaic Covenant's stipulations (Rom. 7:8–9). The covenant also had limited power to provide spiritual life and righteousness for sinful humanity (Heb. 8:7; cf. 7:11; Gal. 3:19–25).

The second covenant, the New Covenant, was also made with Israel. Quoting Jeremiah 31:31, Hebrews 8:8 reads, "Behold, the days are coming, says the LORD, when I will make a new covenant with the house of Israel and with the house of Judah."

The Lord said the New Covenant would be different from the Mosaic Covenant, "not according to the covenant that I made with their fathers in the day when I took them . . . out of . . . Egypt; because they did not continue in My covenant" (v. 9). In other words, when He made the Mosaic Covenant with Israel, the people promised to keep its precepts (cf. Ex. 19:5–8; 24:3–8); but they soon broke this first covenant, committing spiritual infidelity that resulted in God's severe judgment of the nation (Ex. 32; Ezek. 16; Hos. 1:9).

The New Covenant is superior to the Mosaic Covenant because knowledge of God is written on the heart: "I will put My laws in their mind and write them on their hearts" (Heb. 8:10; cf. Jer. 31:33). The Mosaic Covenant was an external code, engraved in stone (Ex. 32:15–16; 2 Cor. 3:7), that promised blessing in exchange for obedience. But the people failed to obey it.

In contrast, the New Covenant is written "on tablets of flesh, that is, of the heart" through the Holy Spirit's ministry (2 Cor. 3:3). All unbelieving Jewish people will experience regeneration at Christ's Second Coming when God pours out His Spirit on the nation. This will result in Israel's repentance and reconciliation with the Messiah (Zech. 12:10; Rom. 11:26). God will give the nation a new heart and spirit (Ezek. 36:26).

With a new heart, no one in Israel will need to teach his neighbor about the Lord because all will know Him, "from the least of them to the greatest of them" (Heb. 8:11; cf. Jer. 31:34). In the Millennial Kingdom, Jewish believers will not require a priest to teach them, for the Lord will teach them through the indwelling Holy Spirit (Isa. 54:13; Jn. 6:45). They will be empowered to walk in His ways and keep His statutes and ordinances (Ezek. 36:27).

The New Covenant is also superior in that it provides forgiveness of sin to those who have been redeemed: "I will be merciful to their unrighteousness, and their sins and their lawless deeds I will remember no more" (Heb. 8:12; cf. Jer. 31:34). The first covenant brought sin to mind with each animal sacrifice (Heb. 10:3). These sacrifices never removed sin; they only covered it (v. 4).

Under the New Covenant, Israel's sins will be remembered "no more" because of Christ's mediatory ministry on Israel's behalf. He was the sacrificial Lamb (Jn. 1:29) who, once for all, took away sin through His blood of the New Covenant (Heb. 10:15–18). The New Covenant gives strong assurance of Israel's forgiveness by use of the term *no more*, meaning "no, never, not under any condition" will God remember Israel's sins (cf. Ezek. 37:23).

Also, unlike the Mosaic Covenant, the New Covenant is eternal (v. 26). This "made the first [covenant] obsolete . . . growing old . . . ready to vanish away" (Heb. 8:13). In other words, the Mosaic Covenant became antiquated, obsolete, useless, inoperative, and was ready to be dissolved with the instituting of the New Covenant. Therefore, the unconditional, eternal New Covenant is superior to the transitory, temporary Mosaic Covenant.

New Covenant Participants

A word needs to be said concerning the parties with whom the New Covenant was made. The text clearly states it was made "with the house of Israel and with the house of Judah" (v. 8). How then does the church relate to the New Covenant?

Some believe God made two New Covenants, one with Israel and another with the church; but nowhere in Scripture are two New Covenants mentioned.

Others believe the church has replaced Israel as the one with whom the New Covenant is made. This view is commonly known as Replacement Theology. It maintains that God replaced Israel with the church because Israel rejected Jesus as its Messiah. Replacement theologians believe the promises originally made with Israel in the New Covenant are now being spiritually fulfilled in the church, which they commonly call "spiritual Israel."

Nowhere is this position taught in Scripture. True, Israel did not receive Jesus at His First Coming, but the numerous promises God made to Israel in the New Covenant were simply postponed, not annulled. These promises will be fulfilled literally and physically to the nation of Israel in the Millennium after Christ's Second Coming.

Still others believe the New Covenant was made with Israel, but it applies to the church as well. Thus there is one covenant but two applications: one for the church now and another for Israel in the Millennial Kingdom. But the church cannot be fulfilling any of the provisions of Israel's New Covenant today because the covenant was made exclusively with Israel and Judah (v. 8), not with the church. Scripture has never called the church Israel or spiritual Israel; and the covenant will be fulfilled in the redeemed nation of Israel after Christ's Second Coming—which precludes it being fulfilled in the church.

Finally, some believe God made only one New Covenant that will be fulfilled eschatologically with Israel, ratified by Christ's blood, but participated in soteriologically by the church today, thus opening the way for Him to bless Jewish and Gentile believers alike spiritually during the Church Age. However, the promised provisions of national, spiritual, and material blessing made to Israel will only be fulfilled to a redeemed Israel during the Millennium. When considering all these possible views, this last one is truest to the teaching of Scripture.

We praise God that a redeemed remnant of Israel will experience the complete fulfillment of the New Covenant blessings during the Millennium.

CHAPTER 13

THE HEBREW TABERNACLE
Hebrews 9:1–10

Christ's high priesthood is superior to the Levitical priesthood because it is based on a New Covenant and operates in a heavenly sanctuary. When referring to the heavenly sanctuary, the author of Hebrews did not speak of the Solomonic Temple (destroyed in 586 B.C.) or the Herodian Temple that was still standing. Instead, he went back to the Tabernacle in the wilderness, which, with its sacrifices and service, originally typified the Lord's ministry in heaven. Since the Tabernacle was merely a shadow of the real sanctuary in heaven, Scripture takes us out of the shadows to reveal in great detail Christ's superior ministry in the heavenly sanctuary. Hebrews 9—10 show that Christ's ministry functions in a new sanctuary with a new service and is based on a once-for-all sacrifice.

Sanctuary of the Tabernacle

The chapter begins by reviewing familiar facts about the Tabernacle's sanctuary and service under the Mosaic Covenant, reminding readers the Hebrew sanctuary was merely a copy of the heavenly one:

> *Then indeed, even the first covenant had ordinances of divine service and the earthly sanctuary. For a tabernacle was prepared: the first part, in which was the lampstand, the table, and the showbread, which is called the sanctuary; and behind the second veil, the part of the tabernacle which is called the Holiest of All, which had the golden censer and the ark of the covenant overlaid on all sides with*

gold, in which were the golden pot that had the manna, Aaron's rod that budded, and the tablets of the covenant; and above it were the cherubim of glory overshadowing the mercy seat. Of these things we cannot now speak in detail (Heb. 9:1–5).

Assuming readers were familiar with the Tabernacle, the author did not mention the courtyard or its surrounding curtain, gate, brazen altar, or laver. He did mention four pieces of furniture used in worship: the lampstand, table of showbread, golden censer, and the Ark of the Covenant. Keep in mind the service mentioned in the first (Mosaic) Covenant was divinely established by God (v. 1) and used by the priests to intercede on behalf of the people.

The Tabernacle proper was 15 feet wide, 45 feet long and 15 feet high. It was divided into two sections: the sanctuary, or holy place, was 15 feet wide and 30 feet long; and the Holiest of All (Holy of Holies) was 15 feet square (vv. 2–3).

The sanctuary contained three pieces of furniture: the lampstand, table of showbread, and gold altar of incense. The lampstand (v. 2, cf. Ex. 25:31–40) stood on the left (south) and was hand-hammered (not made from a mold) from a single talent of pure gold weighing 90 pounds (Ex. 37:17, 24). It had a center stem with three branches on each side, making it seven-pronged.

Light from the huge lampstand filled every corner of the sanctuary with a warm, shimmering brilliance, providing illumination for the priest as he ministered. It was the priest's duty to care for the lampstand. He kept the lamps burning perpetually by filling them daily with pure olive oil (27:20–21). He trimmed each lamp every evening and morning (30:7–8) using pure gold tongs and snuff dishes to collect the used wicks (25:38).

The table for the showbread was made of acacia wood covered with gold (Heb. 9:2). A gold rim encircled its top. Gold rings were placed at each corner, and gold-covered acacia-wood staves were placed through the rings to carry it. The table stood on the right (north) and was three feet long, one and a half feet wide, and two and three-tenths feet high (Ex. 25:23–28). Twelve cakes of unleavened bread containing about six pounds of flour were arranged weekly on the table in two rows of six each in an elaborate service. The bread represented the 12 tribes of Israel. It was called showbread (literally, "bread of the face," or "bread of presence") because it was set before the face, or presence, of Jehovah (who dwelt in the Holy of Holies) as a meal offering from the children of Israel (Lev. 24:8). God gazed with delight on the pure bread offering that sat continually before His face.

The golden altar of incense was 36 inches high and 18 inches square. It was made of acacia wood covered with gold. It had a horn at each corner pointing outward, and a gold rim encircling the top, with gold rings at each corner. Gold-covered acacia-wood staves went through the rings to transport it (Ex. 30:1–4). The altar of incense was actually in the sanctuary in front of the veil (v. 6; 40:5), not in the Holy of Holies. But the high priest filled it with burning incense and took it into the Holy of Holies on the Day of Atonement (Lev. 16:12–13).

The Holy of Holies, which had a huge "second veil" (Heb. 9:3) shielding its entrance, contained only the Ark of the Covenant. The Ark was a rectangular box, three feet nine inches long and two feet three inches wide and high, made of acacia wood overlaid with gold inside and out. It had a gold rim encircling its top, gold rings on the four corners, and staves of gold-covered acacia wood to carry it. The lid, called the mercy seat, was of pure gold. Two cherubim of gold stood on top of the Ark, facing each other. They looked down on the mercy seat, their wings touching, as they stretched out over its top (Ex. 25:10–22).

Hebrews 9:4 states the Ark contained three objects: "the golden pot that had the manna, Aaron's rod that budded, and the tables of the covenant." It has been suggested that a contradiction exists in Scripture because 1 Kings 8:9 says only the tablets of the Law were in the Ark.

But there is no contradiction. Hebrews 9:4 describes the Ark's original contents, while 1 Kings 8:9 records the contents at the time of Solomon's Temple.

After describing the Tabernacle and its furnishings, the author made no mention of the Tabernacle's relationship to or fulfillment in Christ because it was merely a type and shadow of Christ's earthly ministry, which was already completed. Later in the chapter he focused on Christ's ministry in the heavenly sanctuary.

Service of the Tabernacle

Hebrews 9:6–7 briefly describes the service of the sanctuary and Holy of Holies. Priests ministered daily in "the first part [sanctuary] of the tabernacle" (v. 6). Each evening and morning they trimmed and lit the golden lampstand that burned perpetually. They replaced and partook of the showbread every Sabbath, then ate the old bread; and they burned sweet incense evening and morning on the golden altar of incense, the ascending fragrance of which symbolized the worship and prayers of Israel to God.

The high priest alone entered the second room (Holy of Holies) only "once a year, not without blood" (v. 7). He did so on the Day of Atonement (Yom Kippur), the 10th day of Tishri (September/October). Divested of his royal, priestly garments and clothed only in white linen (Lev. 16:4), he parted the huge veil and entered the Holy of Holies to offer blood "for himself and for the people's sins committed in ignorance" (Heb. 9:7). It was necessary that he enter to offer blood, for "without shedding of blood there is no remission" of sin (v. 22; cf. Lev. 17:11).

This was either a day of judgment or life for the people of Israel. If the Lord did not accept the blood atonement, the high priest would die in the Holy of Holies; and the people would not have their sins covered. If the high priest emerged alive, God had accepted the blood atonement for Israel's sin.

Spiritual Significance of the Tabernacle

The Tabernacle, along with its regulations, had been given by direct revelation from God. But it was designed only to be "symbolic [literally, "a parable"] for the present time" (Heb. 9:9). A parable is an earthly story used to illustrate or teach a spiritual truth. The ordered service of the Tabernacle, mediated through the Levitical priesthood, was used as an object lesson in which the Holy Spirit (v. 8) taught the true realities of God to Israel. There are three lessons here:

(1) *Way to God.* The Holy Spirit taught, "The way into the Holiest of All was not yet made manifest while the first tabernacle was still standing" (v. 8). In other words, the way into the Holy of Holies was not disclosed until the inner veil between the two rooms was torn at Christ's crucifixion. After that event, everyone had access through Christ into God's presence. Opening the Holy of Holies was an indication to the Levitical priests that their ministry had been dissolved.

(2) *Worship of God.* The Spirit taught that the Israelites could not be made perfect (brought into a right relationship with God) through the gifts and sacrifices they offered (v. 9). The sacrifices were powerless to remove sin. Thus worshipers experienced no peace but continually had guilty consciences (v. 9).

(3) *Works of the priests' service.* The Spirit also taught that such ordinances as "foods and drinks" and "various washings" were "fleshly" (v. 10). The word *fleshly* does not mean "sinful." Rather, it indicates these sacrificial, ceremonial regulations lacked sufficient value because they removed only external defilement and depended solely on the strength of the flesh. In other words, the Tabernacle and its Levitical sacrificial system were temporary and utterly incapable of bringing the Israelites into a right standing before God.

They were provisionally imposed on Israel "until the time of reformation" (literally, "setting things right, a complete rectification" (v. 10). They could not set things right or restore mankind to a right relationship with God. The Tabernacle and its service were a temporary shadow, external figure, and parable used to represent spiritual truths and point people to a new and better program that God would establish through the ministry of Christ.

A new order was inaugurated when Christ offered Himself as the perfect and final Sacrifice for sin. He fulfilled all the types and shadows mentioned here and made it possible for God to expiate sin. The day of rectification came when the Temple veil was torn in half, opening the way for people to go directly to God through the blood of Christ for the forgiveness of sin. From that day forward, the Levitical system, along with its blood sacrifices, was set aside.

CHAPTER 14

CHRIST'S SUPERIOR MINISTRY
Hebrews 9:11–22

Hebrews 9 begins with a description of the earthly Tabernacle and its ministry through the Levitical priesthood under the first (Mosaic) covenant. Both the Tabernacle and its services were temporary and functioned as an external figure (shadow) to represent spiritual truths pointing people to a new and superior program.

Since the sacrifices were powerless to take away sin, worshipers were continually plagued by a guilty conscience and lack of peace. A new, better program was needed because the Levitical system was insufficient and incapable of bringing the Israelites into a right standing before God. Therefore, God abolished the first covenant and replaced it with an eternal New Covenant implemented through Christ's ministry.

Beginning with verse 9, the book of Hebrews explains the New Covenant's power to remove an individual's sin through Christ's superior ministry.

Christ in a Superior Sanctuary

The phrase *but Christ came as High Priest* (v. 11) is the hinge upon which the argument swings as the author contrasted the old ministry under the Mosaic Covenant and the new ministry under Christ.

The focus is now on Christ's heavenly ministry as "High Priest of the good things to come" (v. 11). These "good things to come" were what Christ accomplished through His more perfect ministry in the heavenly Tabernacle: (1) a better covenant, (2) the purging of a guilty conscience because of sin, (3) personal access and communion with God, and (4) prophetic blessings yet to come.

Christ's ministry functions in a "greater and more perfect tabernacle not made with hands, that is, not of this creation" (v. 11). The Tabernacle Christ entered was not physical or created from earthly materials visible to the human eye. He entered the sanctuary of heaven itself to dwell and serve at the right hand of God the Father. Hebrews 8:2 calls Him "a Minister of the sanctuary and of the true tabernacle which the Lord erected, and not man." Christ functions as High Priest in the very presence of God, making His ministry both effective and meritorious on behalf of mankind, whereas the Levitical system was not.

Christ's Superior Sacrifice

"Not with the blood of goats and calves [bulls], but with [by] His own blood He entered the Most Holy Place [Holy of Holies] once for all, having obtained eternal redemption" (9:12). Christ's shed blood is inestimably superior to the sacrificial blood of animals.

The contrast is between Christ entering by (or through) His own blood and the blood offered by Israel's high priest on the Day of Atonement (Lev. 16). The Aaronic high priest entered the Holy of Holies to offer the blood of a bull for his own sins (v. 11), then he reentered with the blood of a goat for the sins of the people (v. 15). Christ, however, entered the Holy of Holies in heaven by means of His own blood for the sins of humanity.

Did Christ present His blood in heaven? The Greek text does not say He entered "with" His blood but "by" or "through" His blood—that is, by virtue of His atoning work at His death. He entered the heavenly sanctuary, not with literal blood, but with the *blood-right* atonement for mankind's sins. Unlike the Levitical high priest who entered each year to offer animal blood, Christ entered once, there to remain as the Advocate for all believers.

Christ's blood is effective because He is the sinless God-Man. It was

His shed blood that made it possible for Him to enter the Holy of Holies as High Priest; and, on shedding His blood, He purchased and provided redemption for mankind.

Christ's sacrifice was superior to the Levitical system in its sufficiency. He "entered the Most Holy Place [Holy of Holies] once for all, having obtained eternal redemption" (Heb. 9:12). The phrase *having obtained eternal redemption* has a twofold emphasis. First, the Aaronic high priest had to offer animal sacrifices annually on the Day of Atonement for his sins and those of the Israelites. If his offerings were sufficient to remove sin, they would not have been offered annually. In contrast, Christ's once-for-all sacrifice was efficacious and sufficient to provide eternal redemption. He had no sin and, therefore, no need to offer sacrifice for Himself, but only for the people. His one-time sacrifice was sufficient for all who would ever live.

Second, this single act of sacrifice purchased "eternal redemption" for all people everywhere, doing away with the need for an annual atonement in an earthly Tabernacle by a sinful high priest for sinful mankind. However, though Christ's sacrifice provided eternal redemption for all people, it is only efficacious for those who willingly receive Him.

Christ Secured a Superior Sanctification

The Levitical animal sacrifices—such as the sacrifice of "bulls and goats" and the "ashes of a heifer," referring to the ordinance of the red heifer (v. 13; cf. Num. 19)—provided ceremonial cleansing or external purification for the nation of Israel (Heb. 9:13; cf. Lev. 16). These ceremonial cleansings merely purified "the flesh" (Heb. 9:13). If any priest touched a dead body or tomb, he was considered ceremonially unclean and could not enter the Tabernacle for service (Num. 19:13).

The word *unclean* refers to being unhallowed or profane and thus unfit for service. Priests could be brought back into fellowship only through "the blood of bulls and goats and the ashes of a heifer, sprinkling the unclean" (v. 13; cf. Lev. 16:3, 14–15; Num. 19:9–17). The blood of animals merely sanctified (set apart) the priest, making him externally pure and fit to serve in the Tabernacle.

For a man to be cleansed from a sin-ridden, guilty conscience would take much more than external cleansing via animal blood. It would take "the blood of Christ, who through the eternal Spirit offered Himself without spot to God" (Heb. 9:14). Only Christ's shed blood on the cross is able to "cleanse [one's] conscience from dead works to serve the living God" (v. 14).

A number of contrasts can be made between the two types of blood sacrifices:

- Animals themselves are under the sin curse (Gen. 3:14), so their blood can never provide internal cleansing from sin; but the blood of Christ can.

- If the blood of insensible animals, offered involuntarily, could cleanse the flesh from defilement, imagine how much more Christ's blood, offered voluntarily, can cleanse from defilement.

- If beasts without merit (although qualified under Law to be offered for sin) could provide external cleansing, imagine how much more the sinless Christ (who offered Himself to God) can cleanse from sin.

- If the blood of animals purged the Israelites from ceremonial defilement, imagine how much more Christ's blood can purge an individual's conscience from dead works to serve the living God.

- No matter how meticulously the Levitical priests performed their duties, they always bore a sense of guilt and defilement; but in Christ, believers are liberated to experience perfect peace.

Christ's Sacrifice Is Superior in Scope

Because of its nature and type, Christ's blood sacrifice was superior to the animal sacrifices under the first covenant. Through His death, Christ became "the Mediator of the new covenant . . . for the redemption of the transgressions under the first covenant, that those who are called may receive the promise of the eternal inheritance" (Heb. 9:15). Through His death, Christ inaugurated a New Covenant that secured eternal redemption for all believers—those called under the first covenant, as well as those who, in the future, would believe.

The author drove home his point with an illustration: "For where there is a testament [covenant], there must also of necessity be the death of the testator" (v. 16). An inheritance can be acquired only upon the death of the one bequeathing it. The testament in this instance is a covenant that was inaugurated with the death of Christ, through His blood sacrifice on the cross. To activate the covenant, it was absolutely necessary for Christ to die, since He was the one inaugurating it.

Thus the New Covenant could legally take effect only on Christ's death: "For a testament is in force after men are dead, since it has no power at all while the testator lives" (v. 17).

To prove the necessity of blood atonement, the author reminded those contemplating a return to Judaism that even the Mosaic (first) Covenant was inaugurated with blood:

> *Therefore not even the first covenant was dedicated without blood. For when Moses had spoken every precept to all the people according to the law, he took the blood of calves and goats, with water, scarlet wool, and hyssop, and sprinkled both the book itself and all the people, saying, "This is the blood of the covenant which God has commanded you." Then likewise he sprinkled with blood both the tabernacle and all the vessels of the ministry (vv. 18–21).*

Even the first covenant did not become effective until Moses read it to the people, who agreed to keep its precepts (Ex. 24:3–8). Then

Moses sprinkled the book (covenant), people, Tabernacle, and vessels of ministry with blood and water. To become binding, the covenant needed to be ratified by blood because "according to the law almost all things are purified with blood, and without shedding of blood there is no remission [forgiveness of sin]" (Heb. 9:22).

In like manner, Christ has provided for the removal of sin through a New Covenant that He ratified by voluntarily offering, not the blood of animals, but His own uncorrupted blood. He confirmed this truth when, at His final Passover, He declared, "For this is My blood of the new covenant, which is shed for many for the remission of sins" (Mt. 26:28). Therefore, the New Covenant is eternal and unchangeable and provides eternal redemption because it was ratified by Christ alone, who is eternal.

What a wonderful and superior plan God inaugurated through Christ's shed blood for our eternal redemption!

CHAPTER 15

CHRIST'S HEAVENLY MINISTRY
Hebrews 9:23–28

Under the Levitical system, animal blood could only cover sin, never remove it. However, Christ's blood was sufficient and efficacious to redeem mankind and remove sin. The remaining verses of Hebrews 9 show the vast superiority of Christ's New Covenant ministry in heaven over the Levitical priest's ministry on Earth.

Christ Purified Heaven

Christ's ministry reached its culmination in heaven itself: "Therefore it was necessary that the copies of the things in the heavens should be purified with these, but the heavenly things themselves with better sacrifices than these" (v. 23).

The cleansing of the earthly sanctuary is contrasted to cleansing heaven. It was not arbitrary but "necessary" that heavenly things be cleansed by "better sacrifices than these," meaning better than the animals used in the earthly Tabernacle.

The word *copies* refers to the earthly Tabernacle with all its furnishings and ministry. The earthly Tabernacle was only a "copy and shadow" (8:5) of spiritually divine realities in heaven.

The only sacrifice that could cleanse heaven was the one-time sacrifice of Jesus Christ, the perfect Son of God, on the cross. Although the Greek word *sacrifice* is plural, Jesus did not offer many "sacrifices," as mentioned in the text, but only one. Yet His was efficacious enough to fulfill and do away with all the animal sacrifices in the Levitical system.

At this point an issue needs to be addressed. God's sanctuary in heaven is not defiled. He is holy, as is everything that dwells in His presence. So why did the heavenly Tabernacle need to be purified, since all things in heaven are holy? Scripture gives a number of reasons:

First, Satan had access to heaven before and after his rebellion against God (Job 1:6; Isa. 14:12–14; Ezek. 28:11–19; Rev. 12:9–10). Once Satan sinned, he defiled his own sanctuary in heaven (Ezek. 28:18). Thus heaven had to be purified because of his presence.

Second, Jesus' shed blood brought reconciliation to all things, even things in heaven (Col. 1:20).

Third, the works of the unsaved are recorded in books kept in heaven (Rev. 20:12). Thus it is necessary for heaven to be cleansed of all things that speak of sin.

Christ's Presence in Heaven

Hebrews 9:24 describes Jesus' presence in heaven: "Christ has not entered the holy places made with hands, which are copies of the true, but into heaven itself, now to appear in the presence of God for us."

The Tabernacle on Earth was merely a copy of the true Tabernacle in heaven. The Levitical high priest entered the Holy of Holies in the Tabernacle once a year only, on the Day of Atonement, to offer animal blood to atone for Israel's sins. When he did so, he also carried with him hot coals from the altar of incense. The coals produced smoke that filled the room, protecting him from viewing the Shekinah presence of God's glory.

In contrast, Christ entered the heavenly sanctuary to appear before the very presence of God the Father (face to face) on our behalf. The word *appear* (Greek, *emphanisthemai*; v. 24) means "to be manifested." It connotes something manifested or brought about as a result of something new and better. Thus Christ now appears in God's presence with a new and better ministry as our Advocate in heaven.

Scripture further says, "Not that He should offer Himself often, as the high priest enters the Most Holy Place every year with blood of another—He then would have had to suffer often since the foundation of the world; but now, once at the end of the ages, He has appeared to put away sin by the sacrifice of Himself" (vv. 25–26).

The Aaronic high priest entered, not with his own blood, but with the blood of a sacrificed animal. (He could not offer his own blood because it was tainted by sin. And if he had, it would never have been sufficient to cover or take away sin.) The high priest then sprinkled the animal's blood in the Holy of Holies to atone for (cover) his own sins and those of Israel. He repeated this ritual annually because animal blood only *covered* sins for one year; it was unable to remove either his or Israel's sins.

In contrast, Christ did not enter the Holy of Holies of an earthly Tabernacle or Temple but that of heaven itself. There He did not need to offer sacrifices continually, as did the Levitical high priest; He offered Himself only once. For Christ to offer Himself repeatedly as a sacrifice every year (from the foundation of the world) would have been impossible.

The text clearly states, "But now, once [once for all] at the end [consummation] of the ages, He has appeared to put away sin by the sacrifice of Himself" (v. 26). Christ came to Earth as a sacrifice for sin when the past ages of Old Testament history had reached their fulfillment in God's program. Calvary was the one event in history where all the features of God's salvation plan were fulfilled: "But when the fullness of the time had come [the exact historical moment appointed by the Father], God sent forth His Son, born of a woman, born under the law, to redeem those who were under the law, that we might receive the adoption as sons" (Gal. 4:4–5).

The phrase *to put away sin* means to "abolish," or "remove" it. That is, Christ's sacrifice was eternally sufficient and efficacious to remove sin forever. However, though Christ's blood sacrifice has abolished sin forever, it is only applicable for those who repent and trust in Him for salvation.

Christ's Promise From Heaven

On the Day of Atonement, the high priest entered the Holy of Holies to sprinkle blood on the mercy seat for the sins of Israel. During the ceremony, the Israelites waited outside the Tabernacle for the high priest to return from the Holy of Holies. His departure from the Holy of Holies signified to all Israel that his work was finished, his mission was successful, the blood satisfied God, and Israel's sins were covered for another year.

In like manner, after offering Himself as a sacrifice for sin and being resurrected from the dead, Jesus ascended into heaven (Acts 1:11) and remains there as our Advocate before God's throne. At the appointed time, determined by God the Father, He will return to Earth as He promised (Jn. 14:3). His return will signify to all believers the success of His atoning ministry on their behalf in heaven.

Hebrews 9:27–28 states a well-known principle: after death follows judgment. "And as it is appointed for men to die once, but after this the judgment, so Christ was offered once to bear the sins of many."

After a person dies, neither he nor anyone else can present an offering for that individual's sin that could alter his destiny. Death ends a person's opportunity to change his or her position in life; there are no second chances. Nor does anyone die over and over, as taught in reincarnation. A person's earthly life is closed at death, and everyone's eternal destiny is determined and fixed during his or her life here on Earth. From this truth springs a sobering reminder: death irreversibly places people in either heaven or hell based on their acceptance or rejection of Jesus Christ.

Death is an appointment. Everyone dies. Scripture records only a few exceptions. First are Enoch and Elijah. They did not die but were taken directly to heaven (11:5; 2 Ki. 2:11). Second, there will be a generation of believers who will not experience death but will be taken directly to heaven at the Rapture of the church

(1 Cor. 15:51–52; 1 Th. 4:17). Scripture also mentions people who died twice: Lazarus, who was resurrected and died a second time (Jn. 11:43–44), and the people who were resurrected at the time of Jesus' crucifixion (Mt. 27:52–53).

Hebrews 9:27–28 also teaches that Christ was sacrificed one time and died once for the sins of mankind (7:27; 9:12; 10:10). His was a final act that cannot be repeated or reversed. This was a major consideration for the Jewish believers being addressed in Hebrews, as they compared Christ's sacrificial death with the teachings of the Levitical system.

The argument concludes with, "To those who eagerly wait for Him He will appear a second time, apart from sin, for salvation" (9:28). The word *appear* (Greek, *opaw*) means to "behold" and has the idea of Christ revealing Himself to the world at His Second Coming, at which time His promise to return will be fulfilled. At His First Coming, He settled the sin issue once and for all by sacrificing Himself. When He returns He will consummate the believer's redemption and provide all believers with their eternal inheritance as He inaugurates His Kingdom on Earth (v. 15).

Christ's appearance for believers is mentioned three times in 9:24–28. His first appearance was on Earth to become a once-for-all sacrifice by bearing mankind's sin on the cross (v. 26). His second appearance was to minister as our Advocate in heaven (v. 24). His third appearance will be at His Second Coming (v. 28).

As believers, we have much for which to be thankful. Jesus Christ purchased our redemption, removed our sin forever, restored us to fellowship with God the Father, advocates for us in heaven, and has promised us an eternal inheritance at His Second Coming. Hallelujah, what a Savior!

CHAPTER 16

CHRIST'S SUFFICIENT SACRIFICE
Hebrews 10:1–18

Hebrews 10 culminates the central exposition on Christ's eternal priesthood. In his closing argument, the author contrasted the imperfect, insufficient, and ineffective Levitical sacrificial system with Christ's once-for-all, perfect, and sufficient sacrifice (cf. 7:27; 9:12, 26, 28).

This section was meant to convince Jewish believers who were wavering in their faith that the Levitical system was unable to do what Christ did for them.

The Sacrificial System

The Mosaic Law was only "a shadow [outline] of the good things to come, and not the very image [perfect likeness] of the things" (v. 1). At best, it was merely a pale outline and did not provide a true, detailed picture of the sacrifice God would provide through Christ. The Law's sacrifices, offered year after year, could never make the worshipers perfect or righteous in their standing before God.

First, if the worshipers had been perfected (made complete) by a sacrificial offering, then repeated sacrifices for sin would "have ceased to be offered" long ago (v. 2).

Second, if the sacrifices had truly purged (cleansed and kept clean) the Israelites of their sins, the worshipers would have had "no more consciousness [sense] of sins" (v. 2); but these offerings and sacrifices could not take away the consciousness of sin (cf. Heb. 9:9). Therefore, the Israelites never felt free from condemnation. In fact, on the Day of Atonement (Yom Kippur), they continually remembered sin "every year" (v. 3) by offering sacrifices. Thus repetitious offering of animal sacrifices under the Levitical system proved the sacrifices' inability to cleanse from sin.

Israel's sins remained because "it is not possible that the blood of bulls and goats could take away sins" (v. 4). Animal blood had no power to remove sin or provide redemption. It could only cover the Israelites' sin, which then gave them the ceremonial cleansing they needed to approach God in worship (9:13). It was utterly impossible for animals, ignorant of the human moral dilemma and with no control over their own destinies, to remove mankind's sins through their shed blood.

Why then did God establish the elaborate sacrificial system if animal sacrifices could not remove sin? He did so for a number of reasons:

- Blood sacrifices made the Israelites acknowledge their need for atonement before God (cf. Lev. 17:11).
- The sacrifices forced them to admit another must make substitutionary atonement for them; they could not atone for their own sins. Sacrifices were vicarious, substitutionary expiation for their sins, which were symbolically transferred to animals to make atonement and propitiate God's wrath against the sinners. The Old Testament consistently presents God's purpose for sacrifices.
- Sacrifice, which originated in the mind of God, enabled people to have their sins covered before approaching Him in worship.
- The sacrifices pointed to the day when Christ would, once and for all, atone for sin.

In bold contrast to the animal sacrifices that could not remove sin, God's new provision supplies true redemption for mankind. The Son of God came into the world to mediate a New Covenant through the sacrifice of Himself. Not only was the Son involved, but the Father and Holy Spirit also played major roles. Animal sacrifices could never accomplish what the blood of Christ could.

First, it was never God the Father's will for animal sacrifices to remove sin. Two verses make this fact clear: "Sacrifice and offering You did not desire" (Heb. 10:5). "In burnt offerings and sacrifices for sin You had no pleasure" (v. 6). (See also verse 8.) God's displeasure must be understood in a relative rather than an absolute sense. He had commanded Israel to offer sacrifices, and they were to be offered from the heart (1 Sam. 15:22; Ps. 51:16; Isa. 1:11–14). God was pleased Israel offered sacrifices in obedience to His will, but He derived no ultimate pleasure from them because they were unable to remove sin. In contrast, the Son, in dialogue with the Father, stated the means by which He would offer sacrifice for sin: "a body You have prepared for Me" (Heb. 10:5). Through the virgin birth, the Son became flesh with the express purpose of providing redemption for mankind.

Second, it was always the Father's will that the Son become the true sacrifice for sin. The Son Himself said, "Behold, I have come—in the volume of the book it is written of Me—to do Your will, O God" (v. 7; cf. Ps. 40:7). The Hebrew Scriptures are full of Messianic prophecies concerning His First Advent. After His resurrection, Christ said, "These are the words which I spoke to you while I was still with you, that all things must be fulfilled which were written in the Law of Moses and the Prophets and the Psalms concerning Me" (Lk. 24:44). (See Luke 24:27 and John 5:39.) The Father had foreordained "from the foundation of the world" (Rev. 13:8) that His Son would come into the world to remove sin through His death.

Third, Christ was willing to do all of the Father's will: "Behold, I have come to do Your will, O God" (Heb. 10:9; cf. v. 7; Ps. 40:8). With full involvement rather than passive endurance, He actively entered into the work set before Him. He was willing to come as a lowly Babe in Bethlehem, live perfectly under the Law, and suffer the humiliation of a criminal's death on the cross. Christ's own words sum up His commitment: "as the Father gave Me commandment, so I do" (Jn. 14:31). The conclusion is self-evident: "He takes away the first [animal sacrifices] that He may establish the second [Christ's sacrifice]" (Heb.

10:9). Christ's sacrifice was complete, bringing about the demise of the Levitical system.

In obedience to the Father's will, He offered His body as a once-for-all sacrifice, making it possible for mankind to be "sanctified" (v. 10). However, sanctification does not become efficacious until a person puts faith in Him. *Sanctification* means "set apart for God." The concept does not speak of progressive sanctification, which takes place as believers mature, but rather their position in Christ at the moment of salvation. The phrase *we have been sanctified* (v. 10) speaks of a permanent, continuous state believers will enjoy forever.

The Son's Sacrifice

Removal of sin must be implemented through the priesthood. The first covenant priests worked continually: "And every priest stands ministering daily and offering repeatedly the same sacrifices which can never take away sins" (v. 11). Every day, hundreds of priests repeatedly offered ineffectual sacrifices that reminded them of sin but could never utterly remove it. No seat was provided for the ministering priests in either the Tabernacle or Temple, symbolizing that their work was never completed.

In contrast, Christ completed His work as the New Covenant Priest: "But this Man, after He had offered one sacrifice for sins forever, sat down at the right hand of God" (v. 12). Levitical sacrifices were continual; Christ sacrificed once for all. Levitical priests sacrificed animals; Christ offered Himself. Levitical sacrifices only covered sin; Christ's sacrifice removed it. Levitical sacrifices ceased; Christ's sacrifice is efficacious forever.

Today Christ is seated "at the right hand of God" (v. 12; cf. 1:3; 8:1; 12:2), indicating He has completed His work and has been elevated to a position of power and honor. Today He rules with the Father in heaven, "For He must reign till He has put all enemies under His feet"

(1 Cor. 15:25; cf. Ps. 110:1). The "all enemies" are the Devil (Heb. 2:14), the Antichrist (2 Th. 2:8), the False Prophet (Rev. 19:20), and everyone through the centuries who has rejected Christ (Rev. 20:11–15). The expression "till His enemies are made His footstool" (Heb. 10:13) pictures a king standing with one foot on the neck of a vanquished foe, as kings did centuries ago, to show total victory over their enemies. Joshua had his captains do this to the five kings he defeated (Josh. 10:23–24).

Christ is a greater Joshua; He will triumph over the powers of darkness and deliver the Kingdom to the Father at the end of His 1,000-year reign (1 Cor. 15:24–28). Hebrews 10:14 sums up Christ's sacrificial ministry: "For by one offering [i.e., Himself] He has perfected [brought to completion] forever those who are being sanctified" (v. 14). The completeness of His expiatory ministry punctuates the book of Hebrews (2:10; 5:9; 7:19, 28; 10:14; 11:40; 12:23) and stands forever.

The Spirit's Surety

The Holy Spirit witnesses "to us" (10:15) the effectiveness and completeness of Christ's sacrifice in fulfilling the provisions and promises prophesied in the New Covenant (8:8–12; cf. Jer. 31:33–34). With the establishment of the New Covenant through Christ's once-for-all sacrifice, the outward legal code now is written on the heart through an inward change via the new nature of the believer. The Holy Spirit gives believers the capacity to know God's righteousness and live in holiness (Heb. 10:16).

This New Covenant provides complete forgiveness and removal of sin: "their sins and their lawless deeds I will remember no more [no, never, not under any condition]" (v. 17). God purges His memory of believers' sins, making it possible for believers to have a relationship with Him. The Holy Spirit witnesses this fact to believers, thus providing the inner surety of a relationship with God.

One short verse presents the irrefutable conclusion: "Now where there is remission of these, there is no longer an offering for sin" (v. 18). Those who have been redeemed no longer need to offer animal sacrifices. To offer sacrifices for sin would be unscriptural and would show a lack of faith in Christ's finished work. Believers are justified by Christ's once-for-all sacrifice for sin, and they need nothing more.

CHAPTER 17

A LIFESTYLE OF FAITH
Hebrews 10:19–25

To this point, the book of Hebrews has been doctrinal in nature. Using comparison, the author has shown Christ's superiority over angels, Moses, and the Levitical priesthood. He has also shown that Christ's sacrifice on the cross was sufficient to remove sin and provide eternal life to all who believe.

Building on this knowledge, he then set forth the type of life each believer is to live—one of faith, hope, and love.

The Christian's Faith

"Therefore, brethren, having boldness to enter the Holiest by the blood of Jesus, by a new and living way which He consecrated for us, through the veil, that is, His flesh " (Heb. 10:19–20). The word *therefore* looks back to the doctrines taught about Christ in 1:1—10:18 and provides a transition into the practical applications and exhortations in the remaining chapters of the book.

The author addressed his readers as "brethren" (v. 19), indicating they were true believers in Jesus Christ; and he exhorted them to go directly into God's presence with "boldness," meaning freedom of speech and confidence to express their personal needs.

This authority has been granted to every believer on the basis of his or her relationship in Christ. Through His death, Jesus opened for the first time a new and living (life-giving) way for people to come into God's presence (v. 20); "new" because no one could directly enter God's presence under the Law of Moses, and "living" because the way provides life for believers and continual access to God.

Such access was accomplished through the "veil" of Christ's "flesh" (v. 20). At the exact time of Jesus' death on the cross, at the ninth hour (3 p.m., Mt. 27:45), the heavy Temple veil was rent in two (v. 51). Hundreds of people were in the Temple area, as the priests were busy in the Temple preparing the evening sacrifice. Every eye there witnessed this event. Awe and amazement must have struck the priests as they heard and viewed the divine stroke of God tearing the huge veil in half from top to bottom. The empty room of the Holy of Holies stood wide open before them, as if bidding them to come in.

It was at this point that God proclaimed to the Jewish people (and the world) that the ministration of the Jewish priesthood had ended. No longer was a high priest needed to atone for sin annually. Through His atoning blood, Jesus, the true High Priest, had opened the way for mankind to come into God's presence (Heb. 6:19; 9:3–15; 10:19).

The torn veil is a picture of the "torn" body of Christ, who made it possible for us to worship at the throne of God. The same hand that tore the veil in the Temple, from top to bottom, "tore" Jesus' body on our behalf (Isa. 53:10). Although His sacrifice for our sins was (once and for all) offered almost 2,000 years ago, it never grows old but is always fresh and current for all who accept it. His shed blood is a continual fountain, cleansing all who appropriate it for their sin. It provides both a "new and life-giving way."

Christ, who is the only way and life (Jn. 14:6), has made it possible for us to enter God's presence through the "veil" of His flesh. The Temple veil closed off access to all but the high priest who could only pass through once a year. But now, through Jesus' sacrifice, the passage is open to everyone who comes to God by faith in Christ. He changed the veil from a spiritual barrier to a spiritual gateway.

We are also invited to come into God's presence because we have a

"High Priest over the house of God" who bids us to come (Heb. 10:21). The original Greek text actually says "great Priest," recalling the phrase *great High Priest* (4:14) and all that has been said about Christ's exaltation at God's right hand (10:12). Jesus Christ is more than a High Priest; He is the greatest High Priest in history over the actual house of God. No high priest in Israel was ever exalted to such a position.

For Christians, the rent veil means we have a great mediating High Priest who has opened the way for us to have access to the throne of God (1 Tim. 2:5). It also means that, as believer-priests, we can come into God's presence at any time through Jesus Christ with the confidence that we will obtain mercy and find grace to help us in times of need. Since we have this high and holy privilege, we are exhorted to exercise it in four ways:

In a Proper Way. First, "Let us draw near with a true heart in full assurance of faith, having our hearts sprinkled from an evil conscience and our bodies washed with pure water" (Heb. 10:22). This verse reveals four conditions believers must meet before coming into God's presence: We must come with (1) a true heart and (2) assurance, following (3) appropriate preparation and (4) cleansing.

A "true heart" means to come in purity and with truthful motives, gladness, openness of speech, and bold expectation of appropriating all the privileges we have as believer-priests.

"Full assurance of faith [conviction and certainty of faith]" means putting firm trust in God's ability to provide what we ask of Him, without doubting. In other words, we continually are to come before God's throne ready to appropriate an answer to our petition.

We are to draw near, "having our hearts sprinkled from an evil conscience and our bodies washed with pure water." These two concepts are to be understood in the light of the purification rituals required for the high priest on the Day of Atonement. He needed to be properly prepared before approaching God for both service and worship. The high priest had to shed animal blood at the brazen altar and wash his body at the laver before entering the Holy of Holies. Only then could he enter with a pure conscience.

Believer-priests must also experience cleansing—but through Christ's blood—which frees them from an evil conscience of sin. This event takes place when we receive the Lord, wherein we are justified, or declared righteous once and for all, and finally freed from the guilt of sin.

The phrase *bodies washed with pure water* does not refer to water baptism, as many interpret it, but indicates a thoroughness of cleansing through the ongoing process of progressive sanctification after one has been redeemed. At salvation a believer is "washed" and then is progressively being washed through Christ's Word throughout his or her pilgrimage on Earth. The same Greek word is used in the Septuagint for washing the priest for service (Ex. 29:4; Lev. 8:6).

In a Careful Way. Second, we are exhorted to walk carefully before others: "Let us hold fast the confession of our hope without wavering, for He who promised is faithful" (Heb. 10:23). We must "hold fast" (with a tight grip) our confession of Christ, or our Christian commitment, to keep from slipping into sin, coldness of heart, or false doctrine.

Believers are not to waver or bend in their hope as Christians when faced with severe persecution. We must not rely on our own strength but on God's strength through the Holy Spirit, who will give us the stability and immutability to remain strong and committed. The Lord is always near to provide what we need in order to stand. For He said, "I will never leave you nor forsake you" (13:5). God has promised He will not abandon us under any circumstance. Thus we can take great comfort and encouragement in God's promises, which provide strength to stand with a consistent life before a world that opposes our faith.

With Concern for Others. Third, believers are exhorted to have a proper concern for other Christians. We are to encourage one another to live a life of commitment: "And let us consider one another in order to stir up love and good works" (10:24). The word *consider* means to be especially and continuously attentive to the welfare of other believers.

We are continuously to pay close attention to caring for the spiritual, moral, and physical welfare of fellow Christians and stir up, or stimulate, them to lives of love and good works in their walk before fellow believers and the world.

It is clear from this passage that Christians perform a major role in enabling fellow believers to manifest "love" and perform "good works." This task is accomplished through Spirit-filled believers who stir one another to exercise the spiritual gifts given them by the Holy Spirit.

By Assembling With Others. Fourth, we are exhorted not to forsake assembling with other believers: "Not forsaking [abandoning completely] the assembling of ourselves together, as is the manner [custom] of some, but exhorting one another, and so much the more as you see the Day approaching" (v. 25). This verse has both a negative and positive command.

Negatively, Christians may have abandoned the church because of persecution or because they falsely assumed Christ had delayed His return. Or perhaps they stopped attending in order to return to synagogue and Temple worship. Whatever the reason, they are told not to do so; such a departure would discredit their faith.

Many commentators say the words *the Day* refer to Christ's Second Coming, and that well could be. But an argument can be made that the words refer to the coming judgment that would soon fall on Israel when Rome destroyed Herod's Temple and scattered the nation in A.D. 70. Jesus referred to this judgment numerous times near the end of His ministry (Mt. 24:1–2; Lk. 19:41–44; 21:20–24).

Positively, no matter what the conditions might be, believers are to stick with the local church. They are to exhort one another to continue attending faithfully as they "see the Day approaching."

Because of our position in Christ, we have the great and glorious privilege of approaching God directly. This awesome opportunity is not to be taken lightly; it should produce humbleness, a renewed commitment to Christ, and a heart full of praise for what God has granted to us. Come, surrender all, and give Christ the adoration and worship due Him.

CHAPTER 18

WORDS OF WARNING
Hebrews 10:26–39

This section of the book of Hebrews comes on the heels of a strong warning in 10:25 that believers not abandon assembling together, as some were doing.

With judgment approaching, the author provided the fourth of five warnings in Hebrews. This one is much severer than the previous three (cf. 2:1–5; 3:7—4:13; 6:4–8) and is directed to people planning to desert the local congregation and return to the ritualistic system of Judaism. Harsh though it is, it is balanced by a promise of hope and reward to all who remain faithful until Christ returns for His church.

Peril of Rejection

"For if we sin willfully after we have received the knowledge of the truth, there no longer remains a sacrifice for sins, but a certain fearful expectation of judgment, and fiery indignation which will devour the adversaries" (10:26–27). The word *for* connects this section with the previous part of chapter 10 and tells readers why they should heed the warning:

(1) Because they possessed full "knowledge of the truth" they received in Christ.

(2) Because they understood the sin they would be committing. If they proceeded, they would be doing so "willfully," giving forethought to their action and deliberately choosing to pursue sin, no matter what others might say.

(3) Because forsaking the church and returning to Judaism meant embracing a legalistic system that was replaced by the ministry of Christ's heavenly priesthood. The Levitical system they had come out of operated under the Mosaic Law and "no longer [had] a sacrifice for sins" (v. 26). That is, the sacrifices offered under the Law were no longer effective in God's sight because it is Christ's sacrifice that removes sin.

(4) Because forsaking the church meant facing "a certain fearful expectation of judgment, and fiery indignation" (v. 27). Leaving the church to identify with the ritualistic Temple system brought God's judgment on those who returned to a religious system outside of Christ. In this case they were reuniting with a people who would suffer physical judgment from the hand of God.

The author followed his statement with an example from the Mosaic Law: "Anyone who has rejected Moses' law dies without mercy on the testimony of two or three witnesses. Of how much worse punishment, do you suppose, will he be thought worthy who has trampled the Son of God underfoot, counted the blood of the covenant by which he was sanctified a common thing, and insulted the Spirit of grace?" (vv. 28–29).

Under the Law, if a person refused to accept the authority of the Mosaic Law and showed his disdain by deliberately not obeying it, there was no sacrifice offered for, or mercy shown to, that individual. Such a person was convicted on the testimony of two or three witnesses. Once convicted, he was executed by stoning (Dt. 17:4–7).

Although the offense of deliberately rebelling against the Mosaic Law was serious in God's eyes, the offense against Christ and the New Covenant was more serious and deserved greater punishment.

Why? Because this offense rejects the triune God by (1) trampling underfoot God the Father's plan to provide salvation through Christ; (2) counting Christ's blood a common thing; and (3) turning one's back on the Holy Spirit who regenerated, sealed, filled, and baptized that very individual into the body of Christ. This is a great insult.

To count the blood of Christ, through which believers obtain salvation and positional sanctification, as being of less value than the blood of Old Testament sacrifices is a major offense. It is even a worse offense to reidentify with those who reject Jesus as the Messiah and Savior. Such action would align believers with people who completely reject the triune God's plan for salvation.

Quoting from Deuteronomy 32:35–36, the author emphasized that it is God who will judge the apostates: "For we know Him who said, 'Vengeance is Mine, I will repay,' says the Lord. And again, 'The LORD will judge His people'" (Heb. 10:30). He must judge because:

- God cannot look on or overlook sin without taking action on the sinner.
- God's character, righteousness, and holiness demand that He bring judgment on willful sin that is not confessed.
- "Vengeance" belongs only to God who is able to administer judgment rightly and appropriately to fit the rebellious deeds of man.
- People cannot reject God and sin against Him without punishment.
- People deserve judgment. God's judgment is well deserved on those who possess full knowledge of Christ's perfect sacrifice, receive Him as Savior, and then reunite with those who deny Him.

If those being addressed thought they could simply return to Judaism after coming to Christ, they were gravely mistaken. Even in the Old Testament, people who turned away from God experienced His judgment and perished. Verse 31 states, "It is a fearful thing to fall into the hands of the living God."

Falling into the hands of someone means being brought under that person's authority and power. God is fully aware of the spiritual states of all men, especially the hearts and deeds of believers. God is perfect and righteous and will execute absolute justice on all people according to their deeds. "Shall not the Judge of all the earth do right?" (Gen. 18:25). Such sobering words should have awakened any believer and caused him or her not to return to Judaism.

Whether the author had in mind believers who turned back to Judaism after embracing Christianity or believers who only might do so is impossible to know. Most likely the passage warns true believers of the outcome, should they decide to forsake Christ.

Plea to Remember

Readers are alerted to remember a major persecution they suffered at their conversion: "Recall the former days in which, after you were illuminated [enlightened], you endured a great struggle with sufferings" (Heb. 10:32). The word *illuminated* refers to the light of the gospel clearly being perceived, understood, and appropriated, resulting in salvation. They are to "recall" continually the time when they endured severe civil and/or religious persecution when they boldly stood for Christ. Their steadfastness gave evidence of genuine salvation.

These believers suffered for their faith in two ways. First, they "were made a spectacle both by reproaches and tribulations" (v. 33). The word *spectacle* is our word for "theater" and means to be put on stage, as in an amphitheater, and held in derision or mocked and ridiculed with contempt.

Second, they suffered because they were "companions of those who were so treated" (v. 33). That is, they were companions of other Jewish believers, and this fact brought them persecution because of their identification with the church. These Jewish believers were being unjustly mocked by other Jewish people for their commitment to Christ.

Scripture says of these believers, "For you had compassion on me in my chains, and joyfully accepted the plundering of your goods, knowing that you have a better and an enduring possession for yourselves in heaven" (v. 34). They were companions with fellow believers who showed them "compassion" (deep feelings of sympathy) during their imprisonment. They "joyfully" accepted the unjust seizure of their possessions because they knew they had possessions in heaven that were theirs forever. These last two verses provide evidence of their true faith in Jesus Christ.

Promise of Reward

Verse 35 is a direct personal challenge: "Therefore do not cast away your confidence [boldness], which has great reward." The phrase *cast away* means to "fling" or "throw away." The Scripture exhorts them not to throw away the boldness they once had in Christ, as one would throw away an old, worthless garment. In the past, these believers manifested a life of boldness that supported and sustained them during suffering and loss of their possessions. Now they are exhorted and encouraged to exercise the same boldness they had then to sustain themselves through the present crisis that was shaking their faithfulness. They must not throw away their boldness and faith in Christ so as not to lose their "reward" at the judgment seat of Christ.

These believers are told exactly what they need: "For you have need of endurance [patience], so that after you have done the will of God, you may receive the promise" (v. 36). They did not need more faith because, in the past, they had sufficient faith to stand against persecution. What they needed was to exercise their faith with patient endurance to obtain the promise. By doing the "will of God" they would "receive the promise," or the reward, promised at the judgment seat of Christ.

In order to support his point, the author quoted Habakkuk 2:3–4: "For yet a little while, and He who is coming will come and will not tarry. Now the just shall live by faith; but if anyone draws back, My soul has no pleasure in him" (Heb. 10:37–38). Sometimes it seems as if the Lord tarries and delays the fulfillment of His promises, but such is not the case.

In Habakkuk's day, it seemed as if God took no notice of Judah's sin because it went unjudged. But God's judgment was certain; He would use the Babylonians to punish Judah. God has an appointed time to execute His divine plan. In the meantime, "the just [righteous] shall live by faith" (v. 38; cf. Hab. 2:4). In other words, righteous people must live by faith in the midst of persecution and trust that God is faithful to fulfill what He has promised. One who "draws back" in disobedience and unbelief will experience the Lord's displeasure.

The message concludes with an expression of confidence in the Jewish believers to whom the author was writing: "But we are not of those who draw back to perdition [destruction], but of those who believe to the saving of the soul" (v. 39). Because he identified with his readers, we know the author considered them believers in Christ. Those who drew back into Judaism were unsaved. He was confident those he addressed would not forsake the life of faith.

CHAPTER 19

FAITH'S FOUNDATION
Hebrews 11:1–3

Chapter 10 reveals that salvation is established on the bedrock of Christ's sacrifice and not through the Levitical system. Christ's death for sin and His abiding priesthood opened a new and living way for all believers to acquire direct access to God without going through an earthly priesthood. Then, after coming to Christ, believers are to persevere in their new faith. To help them do so, the author paraded a host of men and women from the Old Testament as examples of great faith. By illustrating how their forefathers exercised the same faith in the midst of great persecution, he hoped this generation of Jewish believers would be encouraged to do likewise.

The voluminous testimonies from the lives of these Old Testament saints should speak to the heart of each reader. Many of these Old Testament saints who were faithful to the Lord did not live to receive their rewards, but will receive them in the future. Likewise, these believers must patiently live lives of faith until the Lord rewards them.

Essence of Faith

The author began by describing the distinctives of faith, rather than defining its meaning. He was not specifically referring to the faith one exercises at the time of salvation, although that is included, but faith as a general principle exhibited by a believer as he trusts God for unseen future events in his life.

"Now faith is the substance of things hoped for, the evidence of things not seen" (v. 1). The word *now* looks back to Hebrews 10:38, which functioned as an introduction to the subject of faith in this chapter.

Faith is described by two words, *substance* and *evidence*. The word *substance* (Greek, *hypostasis*) literally means to "stand under," referring to something supporting a foundation, like solid ground standing beneath a foundation. In this context, Christ is the solid ground on which one builds the foundation of his or her faith and hope.

The word *hypostasis* can also be translated "assurance." The Greek term was used in reference to signed papers that gave grounds to prove a person's ownership of a property, thus a legal title-deed giving one assurance and proof of ownership. Therefore, faith functions as the title-deed that gives existence, confidence, or assurance to future events that are "hoped for" from the time of salvation and onward in a Christian's walk. In other words, the act of putting faith in Christ functions as the title-deed that guarantees and assures the believer that God will fulfill all the benefits He promises Christians.

The word *evidence* (Greek, *elegehos*) means to have proof of something through testing it to be true. It can also mean that a believer is inwardly convinced of a thing's reality (i.e., something already finished), which gives him an inner conviction of its certainty although it is a thing "not seen [i.e., not visible to the physical eye]."

Although there are many things concerning God's promises that have already been done for us or are yet to be completed—that we cannot see in our Christian experience—the exercise of faith makes them real to us in the present. These include all the Christian's benefits of salvation, Christ's high priestly ministry, access to God in prayer, understanding how God works through believers' prayers, and how we grow spiritually in our walk with the Lord. The angelic beings in heaven, who are at the beck and call of God to serve and minister to humans on Earth, are another example of things we cannot see (1:14). People of faith believe all these things do exist.

The words *substance* and *evidence* are not to be thought of as independent from each other, but they work together in describing how biblical faith works in a believer's life. True faith, as presented in the Bible, has the inner assurance and conviction that God's Word is true and should be believed and appropriated.

Elders of Faith

In Hebrews 11:2 the author provides a summary statement of men who, in the past, exhibited great faith in the Lord: "For by it the elders obtained a good testimony." The word *for* is used to connect what has been said about faith in verse 1 with upcoming examples of the nature of faith that are to follow throughout the chapter. "By it" literally means "in this," or "by means of this," referring to the sphere and exercise of faith. The word *elders* (Greek, *presbuteroi*) does not refer to old men or men in places of official position, as in a church, but to these believers' Jewish forefathers who were men of faith mentioned in the Old Testament. As the author moves through the chapter, he chooses outstanding men and women of faith as examples to study and follow for the believers he is addressing. These are the great cloud of witnesses mentioned in Hebrews 12:1.

These elders "obtained a good testimony" (11:2). Scholars have interpreted this phrase in different ways. Some believe it refers to the elders receiving approval and praise from God. Others believe that by demonstrating their faith, they experienced the inner witness within themselves that God's Word and promises are true. Still others believe that the faith these forefathers expressed bore testimony to their generation and beyond. This third interpretation is correct: The life these forefathers of faith lived was observed by others, testifying that their faith was genuine.

Evidence of Faith

Although the author might begin by enumerating a list of Old Testament men as examples of faith, he does not. He first takes readers back to before the universe was created, providing one more example of faith: creation itself. This creation illustration helps believers grasp what it means to believe in things that are invisible: "By faith we understand that the worlds were framed by the word of God, so that the things which are seen were not made of things which are visible" (v. 3).

The word *understand* means to perceive by intellectual reflection, not by physical senses like sight. That is, we perceive with our spiritual intelligence that God created the world although we see neither Him nor the act of His creation.

The word referred to as "worlds" literally means "ages" and encompasses much more than the material universe that was created. "Ages" takes in all of time and space; things invisible and visible; the past, the present, and what is eternal. This word includes God's administration of all that exists from its inception to its termination.

God "framed" or outfitted and prepared the universe by making all its parts fit and work together in a harmonious, organized system for His purpose; and He will continually maintain the world throughout the ages. Creation was all done "by the word of God." The term *word* is not the Greek word *logos*, which is used with reference to the Son of God (Jn. 1:1), but *rhema*, which means "utterance." That is, God simply spoke; and creation appeared in six literal days (Gen. 1:1–27). In other words, God didn't create the material universe with anything that previously existed but created it *ex nihilo*, out of nothing.

Since God spoke the material universe into existence out of nothing, it follows that "things which are seen were not made of things which are visible" (Heb. 11:3). A literal Greek translation would be, "so that not out of things which appear hath that which is seen been made." This phrase means that nothing in creation we see today evolved into existence, not even matter; but God simply spoke all things into existence.

The author is arguing, "Had the visible world been formed out of materials which were subject to human observation, there would have been no room for faith. Science could have traced it back to its origin.

Evolution only pushes the statement a stage back. There is still an unseen force that does not submit itself to experimental science, and this is the object of faith."[1]

There are only two positions one can take on creation: Embrace the speculative theories of philosophy or science on how the material world came into being, or accept the explanation from the revelation of God's Word on how the world was created. Whatever position a person chooses to believe, he must accept it on the basis of faith.

All philosophy and science can do is put up plausible theories on how the world was created; but throughout the history of mankind, they have been proven to be false or, at best, pure speculation. God has warned through His Word, "Beware [be on your guard] lest anyone cheat you [carry you off captive or enslave you] through philosophy [vain speculation] and empty [vain, devoid of truth, futile] deceit [trickery or artful deception], according to the tradition of men, according to the basic principles of the world, and not according to Christ" (Col. 2:8).

If a person wants to know what happened at creation, he must by faith totally rely on the invisible God to reveal it to his understanding as presented in Scripture. Is it not a matter of the will to believe or not believe the Bible's revelation on creation? Yes, it is. It's the *only* way to learn the ultimate answers to life's questions on creation and man's destiny.

Endnote

[1] K. S. Wuest, Logos Bible Software edition of Kenneth Wuest's *Word Studies in the Greek New Testament*, 1997.

CHAPTER 20

In Hebrews 11 a gallery of portraits is paraded before us, painted by the hand of God. Each portrait presents the unique faith of individuals who performed great exploits. These men and women believed the unseen. They trusted God's promises; waited patiently for those promises to be fulfilled (rarely receiving them); and refused to allow persecution, pain, prison, or peril to weaken their faith. Neither did they allow disappointment, depression, discouragement, distrust, or the threat of death to crush their devotion to God.

Having described the foundation of faith (vv. 1–3), the chapter then moves us through periods of biblical history to present individuals of faith. Verses 4–7 present three men who lived before the patriarchal period. Although there is only one verse per person, the verses clearly explain why these people are singled out as examples for us to emulate.

Worshiping by Faith

First comes Abel:

> *By faith Abel offered to God a more excellent sacrifice than Cain, through which he obtained witness that he was righteous, God testifying of his gifts; and through it he being dead still speaks* (v. 4).

The story of faith does not begin with Adam and Eve, but with Abel in Genesis 4. Eve gave birth to two sons: Cain, then Abel. Both were born with a sin nature because of the sin natures of Adam and

Eve. One can assume that both were provided with knowledge of God and knew of Adam and Eve's fall. They would have been taught that, by sacrificing animals, God shed blood to provide skins to cover their nakedness (Gen. 3:21).

Genesis 3:21 also shows that people can only approach God if they have a proper covering (one provided by Him), and it reveals explicitly that the covering is not obtained through self-effort but through blood sacrifice. Scripture states (in reverse order of their births) that Abel was a shepherd and Cain was a farmer like his father (4:2).

"In the process of time," Cain brought a fruit offering from the ground, and Abel brought a firstborn sheep from his flock (vv. 3–4). Abel's sacrifice was "more excellent" than Cain's (Heb. 11:4) in three ways: (1) It was a firstborn sheep, (2) it was a blood sacrifice offered by divine decree, and (3) it was presented in faith. On the other hand, Cain's offering was "of the ground" (Gen. 4:3); there is no indication it was the first fruit, was the best of the fruit, or was presented by faith on any altar.

The Lord accepted Abel's offering. Why? Because Abel offered it by faith, as was his duty, and presented it according to God's revealed will. Keep in mind that biblical faith is always tied to God's revealed will. Abel brought a blood sacrifice, the type of offering God required.

In contrast, Cain's offering had no efficacy because it was not a blood sacrifice, nor was it offered in faith. Cain trusted in himself and approached God in his own way, rather than in the way God set forth. Thus God rejected Cain's sacrifice (v. 5).

God told Cain, "If you do well, will you not be accepted? And if you do not do well, sin lies at the door" (v. 7). Rather than return with the proper offering, Cain seethed with anger toward God and eventually murdered Abel.

Abel, however, "obtained witness that he was righteous, God testifying of his gifts" (Heb. 11:4); that is, God received the gift and bore witness that it was correct. It was not Abel's blood sacrifice that made him righteous but, rather, his faith in God (cf. Gen. 15:6). Even a blood sacrifice offered out of duty, not faith, would still be rejected. The proof of Abel's faith was that he brought the right sacrifice in faith and complete obedience to the Lord.

Abel has been dead for centuries, but he still "speaks," or witnesses, to us concerning his life of faith and the need of a blood sacrifice to please God. Abel's witness is that he believed in God, offered the prescribed sacrifice, and was declared righteous and accepted by God because of his faith. What a portrait of faith for future generations to emulate.

Walking by Faith

The second portrait is of Enoch:

> *By faith Enoch was taken away so that he did not see death, 'and was not found, because God had taken [translated] him'; for before he was taken he had this testimony, that he pleased God* (Heb. 11:5).

This is not Enoch from the line of sinful Cain (Gen. 4:17), but Enoch the son of Jared from Seth's line (5:18). Enoch was a man of faith who walked in close communion and fellowship with God. His character and conduct testified against the corrupt, godless age in which he lived. He was a prophet who preached that the Lord would come and judge the ungodly (Jude 14–15). Furthermore, he lived in total obedience to his Lord and "had this testimony, that he pleased God" (Heb. 11:5).

Enoch's end was glorious: "He was not [he disappeared], for God took him" (Gen. 5:24); that is, "Enoch was taken away so that he did not see death" (Heb. 11:5). The word *taken* (Greek, *metatithemi*) means Enoch was "translated," transported suddenly from Earth to heaven. His body was physically changed, and he is now in heaven with a glorified body.

Consequently, it would be impossible for Enoch to be one of the two witnesses in Revelation 11. His translation is a picture of living Christians being raptured to heaven when Christ comes for His church

(1 Th. 4:17). Enoch's removal prior to God's universal judgment on the antediluvian age no doubt prefigures the church's Rapture prior to the future Great Tribulation.

Before Enoch was translated, his character and obedience to God demonstrated that he was righteous. His generation knew of his faith because he had the "testimony, that he pleased God" (Heb. 11:5). Although the Genesis account does not use the word *faith* when speaking of Enoch, Hebrews calls him a man of "faith." Enoch had to be a man of faith or he would not have pleased God.

Verse 6 reveals a universal principle about faith: "But without faith it is impossible to please Him, for he who comes to God must believe that He is, and that He is a rewarder of those who diligently seek Him." Thus individuals who come to God must first believe God "is"—that He exists—and that He eventually will reward those who diligently seek Him. What a testimony Enoch had—one all believers should manifest.

Working by Faith

The third portrait is of Noah:

> *By faith Noah, being divinely warned of things not yet seen, moved with godly fear, prepared an ark for the saving of his household, by which he condemned the world and became heir of the righteousness which is according to faith* (v. 7).

Noah's spiritual qualities and faith are recorded in Genesis 6. He is described as a just man (literally, "justified"), perfect (literally, "blameless" or "having integrity") in his generation. This does not mean Noah was without sin but that he stood complete in his faith. Noah worshiped God like Abel and walked with God like Enoch. Because of Noah's faith, he "found grace [unmerited favor] in the eyes of the LORD" (v. 8).

Hebrews 11:7 records five facts concerning Noah's faith:

(1) *Noah was "divinely warned of things not yet seen."* God told him rain would fall from heaven and flood the whole earth. He instructed Noah on how to prepare an ark so that he and his family could survive the coming judgment. It probably had never rained on Earth (see Genesis 2:5) until the flood. Noah did not argue with God but completely believed the revelation he had received.

(2) *God's revelation produced "godly fear" (reverential awe) in Noah.* He did not doubt God but, rather, was moved by faith to embrace what He had learned.

(3) *Noah "prepared [built and equipped] an ark for the saving of his household."* The ark was more like a huge ship made of gopherwood and measured 450 feet long, 75 feet wide, and 45 feet high. It had three levels, a window in the top, and one door in the side (Gen. 6:14–16); and it was large enough to carry 550 railroad cars of livestock cargo. It was not meant to sail, but float.

Noah likely built the ark during the 120 years when God's Spirit strove with his generation (v. 3). He had only his three sons to help. The ark's purpose was to preserve life during the flood. Noah, his wife, their three sons and their wives, and various species of created life would be saved from death. By faith, Noah obediently built the ark on dry land, with no sea in sight, and probably endured daily scoffing, jeers, criticism, and insults from all who saw him. The people in Noah's day were completely astonished when the flood came. They did not believe judgment was imminent until it swept them all away (Mt. 24:38–39).

(4) *Noah's faith "condemned the world."* The word *world* refers to the ungodly men of Noah's time. Noah's faith in God, his obedience in preparing the ark, his godly conduct, and his preaching of righteousness condemned all those living around him (2 Pet. 2:5). Noah no doubt denounced wickedness and warned people they would face God's imminent judgment unless they repented.

(5) *Noah "became heir of the righteousness which is according to faith."* Noah is the first person in the Bible to be called "perfect," meaning righteous (Gen. 6:9). This term does not mean he was sinless. He was righteous on the basis of his faith in God and because of his commitment to do what God told him to do. Consequently, God imputed righteousness to him. Being an "heir of righteousness" meant he inherited eternal life.

Noah's testimony was that he did "according to all that God commanded him, so he did" (v. 22). Let it be said of us that we worship God like Abel; walk with God like Enoch; and, like Noah, do all God commands of us.

CHAPTER 21

THE FATHER OF FAITH
Hebrews 11:8–22

Now the book of Hebrews moves from the faith of men before the flood to the faith of men in the patriarchal period. The author uses Abraham's faith to illustrate the type of commitment Jewish believers in Christ should emulate.

Submissive Faith

"By faith Abraham obeyed when he was called" by God and immediately left Ur of the Chaldeans, "not knowing where he was going." With his wife, Sarah, and nephew Lot, he traveled to Canaan, which became the land of promise that "he would receive as an inheritance" (Heb. 11:8).

By faith, Abraham settled in this foreign country "with Isaac and Jacob, the heirs with him of the same promise" (v. 9). He lived a nomadic life, dwelling in Shechem, Bethel, Hebron, and Beersheba. The only land Abraham owned in Canaan was the burial plot at Machpelah that he purchased for Sarah (Gen. 23).

Abraham had no permanent house (he lived in a tent) throughout his life because "he waited for the city which has foundations, whose builder and maker is God" (Heb. 11:10). His eyes were not fixed on an earthly city but on a heavenly, eternal one—the New Jerusalem whose architect was God (v. 16; 12:22; 13:14; Rev. 21:1—22:5). Since Abraham's faith was fixed not on his temporal but on his ultimate destiny, he could wait obediently with patient endurance until God's promises to him would be fulfilled.

Keep in mind how great Abraham's faith was: He trusted God totally for the route he would take from Ur; he had no promise of inheriting any land during his journey because God only told him of the land inheritance after he reached Shechem (Gen. 12:6); and though he was promised the land by divine decree, he never took possession of it during his lifetime.

Sarah's Faith

Along with Abraham, Hebrews calls Sarah a person of faith:

> *By faith Sarah herself also received strength to conceive seed, and she bore a child when she was past the age, because she judged Him faithful who had promised. Therefore from one man, and him as good as dead, were born as many as the stars of the sky in multitude—innumerable as the sand which is by the seashore* (Heb. 11:11–12; cf. Gen. 11:29—23:2).

Sarah knew God had revealed to Abraham that He would give him a son. But her faith wavered because she was barren for years and well past the age of childbearing. On hearing the news, she laughed at such a thought (Gen. 18:10–15); but a year later (after Isaac's birth), she laughed with joy. Sarah had exceptional faith to believe she would become pregnant, carry the child to full term, and have the strength to survive childbirth at 90 years of age (17:17).

All commentators consider the phrase *received strength to conceive seed* a difficult text. Scholars take various positions on whether it refers to Abraham receiving strength to impregnate Sarah or Sarah receiving strength to conceive. The first position teaches that Abraham's faith is the subject of the phrase and that he alone caused Sarah to conceive. Because of Abraham's faith, Sarah received "strength" (power) to conceive after menopause. Therefore, God honored the faith of Abraham, not Sarah, in giving him Isaac.

The second position says Sarah is the subject of the verse and that it should be read that, even at her advanced age, she did her part in conceiving a child. Whichever interpretation one takes, Sarah possessed exceptional faith in this situation.

Hebrews 11:12 concludes, "Therefore from one man, and him as good as dead, were born as many as the stars of the sky in multitude—innumerable as the sand which is by the seashore." A number of wonderful applications can be made. First, every Jewish person ever born was conceived because Abraham exercised faith and trust in God's promise. Second, God was willing and able to provide the promised son, but He acted on the basis of Abraham's faith. Third, Abraham did not waver at God's promise but, by faith, claimed the impossible. Fourth, God honored Abraham's faith and gave him a vast multitude of descendants. Fifth, the key to the impossible is faith in God.

Steadfast Faith

In the midst of talking about Abraham and his descendants, the author stopped abruptly to reflect on how these patriarchs lived by faith (Heb. 11:13–16). All of them (Abraham, Isaac, Jacob, and Joseph) died in faith, never receiving the promises given to them—many of which were contained in the Abrahamic Covenant that was passed down to Isaac and Jacob (Gen. 12:1–7; 26:2–5, 24; 28:10–15; 35:9–12; 46:2–4). These men steadfastly clung to the promises, though they saw them "afar off" (Heb. 11:13).

Although the patriarchs could only view these promises from a distance, they "were assured of them, [and] embraced them" (v. 13). Their faith gave them inner conviction that all God promised them would eventually be theirs—if not in their lifetimes, in the generations to follow.

They "confessed that they were strangers and pilgrims on the earth" (v. 13; cf. Gen. 47:9; Ps. 39:12). They had no citizenship in the land in which they lived and "declare[d] plainly that they [sought] a homeland"

(Heb. 11:14), but one much different from Ur in Mesopotamia or the land of Canaan.

Truly, if Abraham had yearned to return to Ur, he had many opportunities to do so (v. 15), but he and his posterity "desire[d] a better, that is, a heavenly country" (v. 16). The word *desire* means to "stretch out, yearn and strive after"; it was a continual, consuming desire that pervaded their lives on Earth.

The patriarchs were steadfast in their faith with a view to the promises of God: "Therefore God is not ashamed to be called their God, for He has prepared a city for them" (v. 16). In other words, Abraham and his posterity did not go back to where they came from or doubt God's promises. Thus God was not ashamed of them, nor were they ashamed to call Him their God. The precise nature of the city they were looking to receive is described in Hebrews 12:22–24 and Revelation 21:1—22:5.

Sacrificing Faith

Abraham's character and faith were tested to the ultimate degree. He was asked to sacrifice his son Isaac: "By faith Abraham, when he was tested, offered up Isaac, and he who had received the promises offered up his only begotten son, of whom it was said, 'In Isaac your seed shall be called,' concluding that God was able to raise him up, even from the dead, from which he also received him in a figurative [parable] sense" (Heb. 11:17–19; cf. Gen. 22:1–19).

God told Abraham to take Isaac to Mount Moriah and sacrifice him as a burnt offering. Although Ishmael (through Hagar) was Abraham's first son, Isaac is identified as "his only begotten son" (Heb. 11:17). This means that Isaac was unique and irreplaceable because he was the only son promised through Sarah and the son who would inherit the covenant promises passed down from Abraham.

The words *offered up* (v. 17) appear twice, first in the perfect then in the imperfect tense. In God's mind, the act of offering Isaac was already completed, and He had already accepted it before Abraham put Isaac on the altar. Abraham's obedience was a great act of faith. He knew God had promised him many descendants through Isaac who was the long-awaited son of promise and miraculous child of his old age. Abraham must have struggled trying to reconcile God's command to offer Isaac and the promise of descendants through Isaac; but neither Genesis nor Hebrews addresses this issue. It seems that Abraham left the problem with God (Rom. 4:20–21).

So convinced was he that God would fulfill His promises that he believed God would raise Isaac from the dead (Heb. 11:19). In fact, Abraham had told his servant, "The lad and I will go yonder and worship, and *we* will come back to you" (Gen. 22:5, emphasis added). Abraham must have been convinced that, if God could birth Isaac through two reproductively dead bodies (Abraham was 100 when Isaac was born), He could raise Isaac from the dead (Heb. 11:12). The phrase *also received him in a figurative sense* (v. 19) means Abraham received Isaac from the dead, not literally but symbolically.

Sons of Faith

The book now moves from Abraham's faith to that of Isaac, Jacob, and Joseph. It mentions incidents near the end of their lives, probably to emphasize that they, like Abraham, trusted God's promises throughout their lives:

- "By faith Isaac blessed Jacob and Esau concerning things to come" (v. 20; cf. Gen. 27:1—28:5). Isaac was a man of faith and believed in God's promises to Abraham his father (Gen. 28:4).
- "By faith Jacob, when he was dying, blessed each of the sons of Joseph" (Heb. 11:21; cf. Gen. 48). Although Jacob blessed all his sons while on his death bed (Gen. 49), the author only mentioned the blessing of Joseph's sons. Jacob knew he would die before God's promises would be

fulfilled, yet by faith he passed the blessing on according to God's will. Both Isaac and Jacob manifested the same faith in the promises given to Abraham.

- "By faith Joseph, when he was dying . . . gave instructions concerning his bones" (Heb. 11:22; cf. Gen. 50:24–26). The author could have illustrated Joseph's faith many ways, but he chose this incident because it clearly shows how strongly Joseph believed God would fulfill the promises made to his forefathers. His request was the same as his father Jacob's, yet he knew he would never live to see the promises fulfilled. During the Exodus, Moses honored Joseph's request and brought his bones up from Egypt (Ex. 13:19; Josh. 24:32).

The men of faith who lived in this period of Israel's history were highly cherished by the Jewish people. During times of persecution, the patriarchs' faith and endurance gave them hope and encouraged them never to give up their faith. The hope was that Jewish believers would emulate these men of faith.

THE FAITH OF MOSES
Hebrews 11:23–29

Moses was a gifted leader whom God used to bring about His plan for Israel and the world. He was blessed with good looks, intelligence, opportunities, eloquence, and leadership ability (Ex. 2:2; Acts 7:20, 22). The Bible describes him as "the man of God" and "the servant of the LORD" (Dt. 33:1; 34:5). In fact, his relationship with God was so intimate that "the LORD spoke to Moses face to face, as a man speaks to his friend" (Ex. 33:11).

His Parents' Faith

"By faith Moses, when he was born, was hidden three months by his parents, because they saw he was a beautiful child; and they were not afraid of the king's command" (Heb. 11:23).

Moses' parents, Amram and Jochebed from the tribe of Levi, were people of faith (Num. 26:59). Moses was born in Egypt in an era when the midwives were under orders to kill all Jewish newborn males (Ex. 1:15–17).

Moses is described as a "beautiful [i.e., good] child" (Heb. 11:23; cf. Ex. 2:2; Acts 7:20). Perhaps his parents were aware that Israel's 400-year captivity in Egypt (Gen. 15:13–14) was soon to end and that their son might play a role in Israel's deliverance. Whatever the reason, they demonstrated faith in God and hid Moses for three months.

When Jochebed could no longer hide him, by faith she made an ark of bulrushes, daubed it with asphalt and pitch, and laid Moses in it by the riverbank. Pharaoh's daughter (possibly Hatshepsut, the young daughter of Thothmes I) discovered the infant and asked Moses' sister, Miriam, waiting nearby, to summon a Hebrew nurse.

In God's sovereignty, Jochebed became his nurse. Pharaoh's daughter gave Moses to his mother and even paid her wages until he became Pharaoh's daughter's adopted son (Ex. 2:1–10; Acts 7:21).

Thus Jochebed had a number of years to implant in Moses a sense of his Jewish identity. This is a beautiful example of how God honored the faith of a humble, God-fearing couple. He answered their prayer, spared Moses' life, and fulfilled His purpose for him.

His Personal Faith

Moses' life is divided into three major sections of 40 years each. The first 40 years were spent in Pharaoh's court; the second 40, in the desert of Midian; and the last 40, in the desert of Sinai.

> *History provides some insight concerning the royal court at that time:*
>
> *Scholars tell us that this Pharaoh had a son, who because he was physically and mentally handicapped, was considered incapable of assuming the royal prerogatives to which he had been born. When he ascended the throne as Thothmes II, his sister Hatshepsut became regent and actually ruled the country. Thothmes II eventually died without a legitimate heir, but because both his father and sister had foreseen this lack of a successor, they probably had determined long beforehand that Moses would be the eventual heir. So from earliest years Moses had been educated with this in mind, as Stephen declares: "Moses was learned in all the wisdom of the Egyptians, and was mighty in words and deeds" (Acts 7:22).*
>
> *When her brother died, it appears that Hatshepsut retained supreme authority as regent in Egypt and indicated her intention of placing Moses, her adopted son, on the throne as her successor.*

> *To legitimize this, she had planned to marry Moses to her elder*
> *daughter, Nepherus. Moses, however, apparently both refused the*
> *throne and the bride, and thus sacrificed his position in the kingdom*
> *and the honor and the wealth that went with it.*[1]

A number of steps were involved in Moses' journey of faith:

Rejection. First, Moses rejected his royal position: "By faith Moses, when he became of age [40 years old, Acts 7:23], refused to be called the son of Pharaoh's daughter" (Heb. 11:24). This decision was an act of faith. He chose to leave his royal privilege in Egypt and identify with the Israelite slaves (Ex. 1:8–14).

Reevaluation. Moses chose "rather to suffer affliction with the people of God" (Heb. 11:25). He viewed Israel not as slaves, but as God's people. He knew the Lord had called him to be part of his people's divine destiny and was willing to suffer affliction with them.

Refusal. Moses refused to "enjoy the passing pleasures of sin" (v. 25). His royal position offered him all the enjoyment and experiences of prestige and power that most men want. However, Moses shunned them all. For him to remain in Egypt's court would have been the sin of disobedience because he knew God was calling him to a divine mission among the Israelites.

As the text says, sin is a "passing pleasure"; it provides only momentary satisfaction that is deceptive and fleeting. The patriarch Joseph had a royal position in Egypt for many years and remained a godly man, serving God in total commitment. The same could be said of the prophet Daniel, who enjoyed royal privileges in Babylon.

Reflection. Moses was well aware of the reproach he would suffer. He did not jump quickly to leave the royal court but carefully reflected on what it would cost him before making his life-changing decision. He was willing to suffer "reproach" (v. 26)—to be derided, laughed at, and persecuted for his choice.

Scripture puts Moses' decision into a Christian context: "esteeming [considering] the reproach of Christ greater riches than the treasures in Egypt" (v. 26). The word *Christ* is the same as *Messiah* and means "Anointed One." Some believe verse 26 means Moses experienced the same type of rejection and persecution as Christ. Others believe it means Christ was with Israel and Moses during their suffering and that He suffered along with them (cf. Isa. 63:9).

Still others believe the phrase refers to the reproach Moses bore because of his relationship to the promised Messiah and, by faith, anticipated it would come.

What we do know is that God revealed much to Moses about a coming prophet who would later be identified as Jesus Christ. (See Deuteronomy 18:15–19 and John 5:46.) Thus he probably knew more about Christ than Abraham before him (Jn. 8:56). It is not unreasonable to believe that Moses, being a deliverer of God's people, suffered the same type of rejection and reproach from his people as would Jesus, the coming Messiah.

Moses considered what he had in the Messiah (Christ) to be "greater riches than the treasures in Egypt" (Heb. 11:26). Wrote Bible expositor Homer Kent: "The wealth and opulence of the Eighteenth Dynasty is well known from the remains of tombs and temples. The fabulous treasures discovered in the tomb of Tutankhamen, a later pharaoh in this dynasty, speak eloquently of the luxuries available to royalty in Egypt."[2] Moses gave up great wealth for the greater wealth he had in Christ.

Reward. Moses knew he would be rewarded for his faith, and "he looked to the reward" (v. 26). He did not look for earthly wealth and opulence but, rather, for spiritual wealth that was eternal and would be granted in the life to come.

His Public Faith

Moses exhibited persevering faith: "By faith he forsook [abandoned]

Egypt, not fearing the wrath of the king" (v. 27). Moses left Egypt twice: when he fled to Midian and when he led Israel out of Egypt. Many commentators believe Hebrews 11:27 refers to Moses fleeing Midian because the word *he* seems to fit that occasion better. But the verse states that Moses left not fearing the king's wrath. When Moses fled to Midian, he did so in fear, not in faith (Ex. 2:14–15).

In the Exodus, Moses "forsook" or permanently departed from Egypt, totally renouncing it. This was not the case in going to Midian. So it seems best to interpret the passage as referring to when Moses left in the Exodus.

Moses departed Egypt strong in faith because "he endured [held fast and persevered] as seeing Him who is invisible" (Heb. 11:27). With no means to defend Israel against Pharaoh, Moses persevered, keeping his eyes fixed on the invisible God who enabled him to stand boldly against the exceedingly great power of Pharaoh, who was determined to destroy him and keep the Israelites in slavery.

Moses exhibited faith by instituting the Passover: "By faith he kept the Passover and the sprinkling of blood, lest he who destroyed the firstborn should touch them" (v. 28). In obedience to God's command, Moses instructed each Israelite household to kill a lamb and apply some of its blood to the lintels and doorposts of their houses to protect them from physical death. For God was to pass through Egypt, killing the firstborn of man and beast in each house not protected by the blood (Ex. 11:4; 12:12–13, 23, 27, 29). Moses' faith in God's provision of blood protection was great indeed because neither he nor Israel nor the world had ever seen such deliverance.

Moses exhibited faith in God's protection: "By faith they passed through the Red Sea as by dry land, whereas the Egyptians, attempting to do so, were drowned" (Heb. 11:29).

The Red Sea crossing is recorded in Exodus 14. Pharaoh pursued Israel hoping to recapture his slaves. The Israelites, struck with terror, were trapped by the sea in front and Pharaoh's army at the rear. Frightened and angry, they blamed Moses for their predicament. In a step of great faith, Moses declared, "Do not be afraid. Stand still, and see the salvation of the LORD. . . . For the Egyptians whom you see today, you shall see again no more forever. The LORD will fight for you, and you shall hold your peace" (Ex. 14:13–14).

As the children of Israel walked into the sea, the waters parted; and they walked on dry land with the water walled up on both sides. The Egyptians tried to follow and drowned in the sea (vv. 27–28). God had promised to protect and deliver Israel, but both Moses and Israel had to step out in faith.

Moses stands as a giant when it comes to faith, character, and resolve to serve the Lord. The lessons we can learn from his faith should strengthen our faith as well.

Endnotes

1 J. Dwight Pentecost, *Faith That Endures*, devotional notes by Ken Durham, rev. ed. (Grand Rapids, MI: Kregel, 2000), 188–189.

2 Homer A. Kent, Jr., *The Epistle to the Hebrews* (1972; reprint. Winona Lake, IN: BMH Books, 2002), 239.

CHAPTER 23

FAITH AT JERICHO
Hebrews 11:30–31

After 400 years in Egyptian captivity, the Israelites prepared to enter the Promised Land. The Lord commanded Moses to send one representative from each of the 12 tribes to search out the land of Canaan. Ten of the spies returned with a bad report and plunged the nation into sin: "We are not able to go up against the people, for they are stronger than we . . . and we were like grasshoppers in our own sight" (Num. 13:31–33). Only Joshua and Caleb had faith in both God's promise and power to deliver the land to Israel (14:6–8).

The Lord pardoned Israel's sin of unbelief, but He made the nation wander 40 years in the wilderness until the generation coming out of Egypt died (vv. 20–38). Only Caleb and Joshua survived.

Hebrews 11 says nothing of Israel's wilderness wandering and jumps directly from the Red Sea crossing (v. 29) to the nation's exercise of faith at Jericho (v. 30)—probably because Israel exhibited little faith during its 40 years in the desert.

A Commander's Faith

Though Hebrews does not mention Joshua, he was a tower of faith in Israel's odyssey. His character was impeccable, never marred by scandal or sin during the years he served the Lord under Moses. His life, in fact, is filled with lessons on how to live vigorously and victoriously by faith.

Joshua was selected to serve Moses as a leader during Israel's wilderness wandering. He was with Moses on Mount Sinai (Ex. 24:13), and he faithfully submitted to Moses' leadership until Moses died. Joshua was also a soldier, chosen by Moses to lead Israel in vanquishing the Amalekites (17:8–16). God chose Joshua to succeed Moses, and Moses charged Joshua to be a strong and courageous leader because God promised to use him to bring Israel into the Promised Land (Dt. 31:14, 23).

For the task, God gave Joshua supernatural skills, empowering him by filling him with the "spirit of wisdom" (34:9). Joshua implemented the spiritual strategy God gave him, waiting patiently until God parted the Jordan River so that Israel could cross into the land. Once there, he circumcised the men, kept the Passover, and received divine instructions from the Commander of the Lord's army before invading Jericho (Josh. 5).

A Conquering Faith

Concerning Jericho's destruction, Hebrews briefly states, "By faith the walls of Jericho fell down after they were encircled for seven days" (11:30). Jericho is 853 feet below sea level. It is located four miles west of the Jordan River and is known as the City of Palm Trees. The many springs around Jericho make it ideal for habitation. In Joshua's day, Jericho was considered a frontier town and the key city to the land of Canaan after crossing the Jordan River.

It was absolutely mandatory that Israel conquer Jericho if it were to take possession of the Promised Land. Humanly speaking, the city's massive walls and heavily equipped army would have seemed invincible and immune to attack by an untrained horde of men who had spent 40 years wandering the Sinai Desert. But the real impediment to victory was spiritual: Would Israel put complete trust in God to provide it with the right plan, wisdom, and strength to conquer Jericho?

The story of the city's fall under Joshua is described in Joshua 6. When the Israelites arrived they found Jericho securely shut up because it greatly feared Israel.

The Lord gave Israel a plan for conquering the city once the huge walls collapsed. He promised Joshua that He had given Jericho, its king, and its mighty men to Israel. All Israel had to do was exercise faith in God's plan and be obedient to what He required of them.

So God instructed the Israelites to march around Jericho in silence once a day for six days. On the seventh day they were to march around the city seven times. On the seventh day, seven priests marched around Jericho before the Ark of the Covenant, with a shofar in hand. Then, at a given signal, the priests blew the shofar with one long blast. The people, who previously had been silent, shouted loudly; and the mighty walls of Jericho collapsed. Then the Israelites attacked the city and destroyed all the people, oxen, sheep, and donkeys (Josh. 6:1–5, 20–21).

The new generation was different from the one that came out of Egypt. It was full of faith, believing it could take Jericho. These Israelites put their future into God's hands, and He honored their faith by giving them Jericho.

A Courageous Faith

With the stroke of his pen the author of Hebrews almost shocks us by including the story of a Jericho harlot named Rahab: "By faith the harlot Rahab did not perish with those who did not believe, when she had received the spies with peace" (Heb. 11:31).

Rahab's faith manifested itself before Jericho's destruction (Josh. 2). Before taking the city, Joshua sent two men there on a reconnaissance mission. They lodged at Rahab's house, located on the city's wall. When the king of Jericho heard they were there, he sent men to capture them. So Rahab quickly hid them under flax on her roof.

She admitted to the king's emissary that the spies had come, but she also said they had already fled. After the spies promised that the Israelites would spare Rahab and her family after they conquered Jericho, Rahab helped the spies escape. She told them to hide in the mountains for three days until their pursuers gave up the search.

The men told Rahab to bring all her relatives into her house and to tie a scarlet cord in the window; she and all in her house would be spared. During the invasion, the spies kept their word: "And Joshua spared Rahab the harlot, her father's household, and all that she had. So she dwells in Israel to this day, because she hid the messengers whom Joshua sent to spy out Jericho" (6:25).

Many people wonder how God could use a prostitute to accomplish His will. Some have suggested that Rahab was not actually a prostitute but an innkeeper or a hostess. However, the text clearly calls her a harlot. Rahab is not praised for what she was but for her great faith in God within a pagan culture. There also is no indication she continued her wicked life as a harlot after becoming identified with Israel.

It is hard to believe that a person like Rahab, an Amorite living in a totally pagan society apart from the covenant promises of Israel, could have exercised such great faith. Herein lies a supreme example of God's mercy and grace. He is able to reach down and save the most unlikely person, even someone whom most people of faith would deem hopelessly lost.

Joshua 2 reveals that Rahab had knowledge of Jehovah God. She was well-informed concerning Israel's recent history and miraculous deliverance from Egypt. How she heard the news of God's grace, mercy, and mighty miracles is unknown. The important point is that she believed it. Rahab's faith and belief in God, like Abraham before her, was imputed to her for righteousness.

A few examples of Rahab's faith are recorded in Hebrews and Joshua. She "received the spies with peace" at the peril of her own life (Heb. 11:31). James wrote, "Likewise, was not Rahab the harlot also justified by works [meaning her works proved that she was a believer] when she received the messengers and sent them out another way?" (Jas. 2:25).

Rahab declared her faith when she used the word *Lord* (Josh. 2:9), meaning "Jehovah," speaking of the one true God of Israel.

- She saw Jehovah as the personal God of Israel when she called Him "your God" (v. 11).
- She believed Jehovah who had given the Israelites the land (v. 9).
- She believed in God's divine redemptive power that miraculously delivered Israel at the Red Sea and from two Amorite kings (v. 10).
- She believed Jehovah to be the only true God who ruled over "heaven above and on earth beneath" (v. 11).
- She believed God would spare and deliver her and her father's household (vv. 12–13).
- She trusted the two spies and obediently followed their instructions (v. 21).
- She was steadfast in her faith, exhibiting full assurance that Israel would defeat and capture Jericho.

God protected Rahab because of her faith, and she "did not perish with those who did not believe" (Heb. 11:31). Her faith secured her a great reward and her family a place in Israel with the people of God (Josh. 6:25). She is included in the Messianic line of Jesus Christ: "Salmon begot Boaz by Rahab, Boaz begot Obed by Ruth, Obed begot Jesse, and Jesse begot David the king" (Mt. 1:5–6; cf. Ruth 4:21–22)—all in the lineage of Jesus Christ.

Both Israel's victory over Jericho and Rahab's deliverance prove God extends His mercy, grace, and salvation to anyone who exercises true faith in seeking Him.

CHAPTER 24

THE ACCOMPLISHMENTS OF FAITH
Hebrews 11:32–40

The beginning of Hebrews 11 describes faith. Then it systematically illustrates it in the lives of those who lived before the patriarchal period until Israel crossed the Jordan River into the Promised Land (vv. 1–31). Then the author expressed his quandary: "What more shall I say? For the time would fail me to tell" (v. 32).

To mention all the faithful individuals in Israel's history would be too time-consuming. Thus, for the remaining verses of chapter 11, he selected a few faithful individuals to illustrate that the principle of faith was manifested through Israel's history.

Six men of faith from the period of the judges, kings, and prophets are listed out of chronological order. In the Old Testament, Barak precedes Gideon, Jephthah precedes Samson, and Samuel precedes David. Scripture does not say why these men were chosen or why they were presented in this order (v. 32).

We do know they were ordinary men whom God called on to accomplish extraordinary feats of faith after being endowed and energized by the Holy Spirit. These men appear in verse 32 exclusively because of their faith.

People of Faith

Gideon (cf. Jud. 6—9). The Lord sent Gideon to save Israel, which was groaning under Midianite oppression (6:14). God's plan was to defeat the Midianites with a mere 300 Israelite soldiers. Against overwhelming odds, Gideon put unwavering faith in God's plan and power and defeated the Midianite coalition of 135,000 men. In confusion, the Midianites fought one another and eventually fled from the Israelites (7:1–25; 8:10).

Barak (cf. Jud. 4—5). King Jabin of Canaan had suppressed Israel for 20 years, and the nation cried out to God for deliverance. The Lord promised Deborah, the judge of Israel, that she would defeat Sisera, the captain of Jabin's army, who had 900 iron chariots under his command. The Lord told Deborah to ask an obscure man named Barak to muster an army of 10,000 men from the tribes of Naphtali and Zebulun, assemble them atop Mount Tabor, and charge down the mountain. There the Lord would defeat the Canaanites.

Many believe it was Deborah, not Barak, who had faith to believe Israel would triumph. Not so. Barak was a fearless warrior of faith who willingly fought Sisera. Barak wanted Deborah with him, not because he was fearful, but for her spiritual wisdom and direction as the Lord's spokesperson (4:1–24).

Samson (cf. Jud. 13—16). Samson was a judge in Israel who was given a special mission: Oppose the Philistines oppressing Israel. He is best known, not for his faith, but for his physical strength, immaturity, self-will, self-confidence, and foolishness in trusting the pagan woman Delilah who brought him down. Nevertheless, God used him in many situations to defeat the Philistines. On those occasions, Samson exercised faith in God to perform mighty acts, never doubting that his power and strength came from God.

Jephthah (cf. Jud. 11—13). Jephthah, the son of a harlot, became a soldier of fortune whom God later selected to be a judge to fight the Ammonites. Despite his downfall by making an awful vow, Jephthah was a man of faith. He trusted totally in God's power, manifested great faith in the Lord, and believed he would be victorious over the Ammonites.

David. King David exercised great faith when he killed a lion, a bear, and the Philistine giant Goliath. His faith never wavered when he ran from Saul, who sought his life; faced rebellion within his own family; and directed and fought wars while king. Despite his gross sins of adultery and murder, God called him "a man after My own heart, who will do all My will" (Acts 13:22; cf. 1 Sam. 13—22).

Samuel. Samuel was called as a child to be a priest and prophet. Later he became the last judge over Israel (1 Sam. 3:10, 20–21; 7:15–17). He exercised great faith, standing against Israel's enemies (Philistines, Amorites, and Ammonites) and courageously opposing King Saul, who was disobedient to the Lord. While Saul was still in office, Samuel exercised faith in anointing David to be king (13:1–14; 16:1–2, 12–13).

Prophets. There were many prophets of faith in Israel, but the author did not list them.

Persecution of the Faithful

In quick succession, Scripture lists many great examples of faith, even during persecution, but does not name names.

Triumphs of Faith (Heb. 11:33–35)

- *Subdued kingdoms:* Gideon, Barak, Samson, Jephthah, and David.
- *Worked [performed acts of] righteousness:* Through faith they walked uprightly and lived righteously. Samuel and the prophets were such examples.
- *Obtained promises:* What God promised He provided, especially specific victories over Israel's enemies, as promised to Gideon, Barak, and David.
- *Stopped the mouths of lions:* This was true of Samson (Jud. 14:5–6), David (1 Sam. 17:34–36), and Daniel (Dan. 6:16–23).
- *Quenched the violence of fire:* Shadrach, Meshach, and Abed-Nego survived in King Nebuchadnezzar's fiery furnace (Dan. 3).
- *Escaped the edge of the sword:* Many within Israel escaped being killed by adversaries, including Moses (Ex. 18:4), Elijah (1 Ki. 19:1–3), and Elisha (2 Ki. 6:31).

- *Out of weakness were made strong:* Gideon (Jud. 6:14–16), Samson (16:30), and David (1 Sam. 17) all were weak but by faith were made strong.
- *Became valiant [brave] in battle [and] turned to flight the armies of the aliens:* Such was true of Joshua, some judges, and especially King David.
- *Women received their dead raised to life again:* Elijah raised from the dead the son of the woman of Zarephath (1 Ki. 17:17–24), and Elisha raised the son of a Shunammite woman (2 Ki. 4:18–37).

Trials of Faith (Heb. 11:35–37)

- *Others were tortured, not accepting deliverance, that they might obtain a better resurrection:* The word *tortured* (Greek, *tumpanizo*) means to "to beat a drum"; thus the torture involved being beaten. The tympanum as an instrument of torture seems to have been a wheel-shaped frame upon which criminals were stretched and beaten with clubs or leather whips.
- The Greek text reads "the deliverance," referring to a specific deliverance offered to Christians if they would deny their faith. However, those being tortured refused the offer because they looked to "obtain a better resurrection" (v. 35). They preferred to die, rather than renounce Christ, knowing they would experience eternal life in their resurrected bodies.
- *Others had trial of mockings and scourgings . . . chains and imprisonment:* Many Old Testament prophets experienced such persecution, particularly from their own countrymen. Yet they never wavered in their faith or commitment, nor did they compromise the message God asked them to deliver.
- *They were stoned:* Stoning was Israel's usual form of capital punishment. Zechariah, the son of Jehoiada, likely was stoned to death (2 Chr. 24:20–22), as was Stephen who was falsely accused of blasphemy (Acts 7:55–60).

- *They were sawn in two:* Jewish tradition has taught that Isaiah the prophet died by being sawed in half.

- *Were tempted:* Satan tempted believers with discouragement and doubt when they were called on to exercise faith. Moses was tempted with position, wealth, and the pleasures of sin before he left Pharaoh's court in Egypt. Job was tempted to doubt God because of his suffering, and Daniel was tempted to compromise his faith while a captive in Babylon.

- *Were slain with the sword:* Elijah said Israel slew its prophets with the sword (1 Ki. 19:10). Evil Queen Jezebel had many prophets slain (18:4). Herod Agrippa had James slain by the sword (Acts 12:2).

- *They wandered about in sheepskins and goatskins, being destitute, afflicted, tormented:* Men and women of faith became outcasts. Elijah wore goatskins. Often prophets in Israel were destitute, afflicted, and tormented physically and verbally.

- *They wandered in deserts and mountains, in dens and caves of the earth:* This fact was true of 100 prophets whom Obadiah saved from Jezebel's wrath by hiding them in two caves (1 Ki. 18:4). Many people of faith experienced such things through the centuries.

Scripture describes these people as individuals "of whom the world was not worthy" (Heb. 11:38). The world had no use for people of faith and poured contempt on those who were forced to flee their godless persecutors. Some believers had to live in caves and the desert.

Promise to the Faithful

The author then summarized chapter 11. First, the faithful received God's approval because they "obtained a good testimony through faith" (v. 39). They demonstrated that believers can live lives of faith and will be rewarded by God. The list in Hebrews 11 is merely a sampling of godly people in the Old Testament.

Second, these faithful anticipated receiving what God had promised but "did not receive the promise" (v. 39). Old Testament believers looked for a Messiah who would provide a Messianic Kingdom filled with national and spiritual blessing. Although they never saw the Kingdom in their day, they died in faith believing God would do what He promised.

Then the author drove home his application: "God having provided something better for us, that they should not be made perfect apart from us" (v. 40). The Old Testament saints received promises from God because of their faith, but they did not receive the promise apart from us. In other words, the promise of salvation and the Messianic Kingdom for all believers could not be completed until after Christ's death and resurrection. Old and New Testament believers will be made "perfect" (complete, v. 40) at the same time: at their glorification and return to Earth at Christ's Second Coming.

The testimony of the Old Testament faithful is an appeal to all believers, especially first-century Jewish believers who were considering a return to Judaism because of persecution. Instead, they were to take heart and exercise greater faith in God's promises because they had greater revelation in the resurrected Messiah.

Hebrews 11 illustrates how men and women in ages past exercised great faith despite their circumstances and were triumphant. We should emulate their faith and, like them, with patient endurance, stand firm in our commitment to the Lord no matter what the cost.

CHAPTER 25

A FAITH THAT ENDURES
Hebrews 12:1–4

The book of Hebrews was written to provide evidence of Jesus Christ's divinity, confirm that the Mosaic Law had been both fulfilled and abrogated in Christ, and exhort Jewish believers to remain steadfast in their faith and continue to spiritual maturity.

Three times in the first three verses of Hebrews 12, Jewish believers are commanded to endure persecution patiently for their faith in Christ. To encourage them not to vacillate, the author provided two examples of those who endured persecution. First, he mentioned Old Testament believers who exemplified living by faith. Then he provided the supreme example: Jesus Christ, who was faithful even to death.

Prior Encouragement

The chapter begins with a word of encouragement:

> *Therefore we also, since we are surrounded by so great a cloud of witnesses, let us lay aside every weight, and the sin which so easily ensnares us, and let us run with endurance the race that is set before us* (v. 1).

The word *cloud* is used metaphorically to speak of a huge group of believers in heaven. The word *witness* (Greek, *marturon*) means one who testifies to what he has seen, heard, or knows personally. In the first century, it referred to someone who witnessed the signing of a contract or legal document. Thus the phrase *cloud of witnesses* refers to those cited in Hebrews 11 as examples of faith throughout Jewish history. These Old Testament believers were approved by God because of their faith. Thus they showed the early church the type of faith that pleases God.

All believers, especially during times of persecution, should study the lives of these men and women, be greatly encouraged by them, and emulate their faith. They were able to endure, and we must do likewise.

A word must be said about what the phrase *cloud of witnesses* does not mean. It does not mean these "witnesses" are looking down from heaven on believers and know how they are living out their faith. Often Christians find comfort in thinking their loved ones can see them and know the struggles they face here. These may be nice thoughts, but Scripture does not contain this teaching.

Practical Exhortation

The author used the concept of a foot race to illustrate the type of faith believers should have. The word *race* (Greek, *agona*) is the English word for "agony" (v. 1). Pictured here are runners in a marathon, like those in the Grecian games. The race was an agonizing, grueling ordeal; and winning required self-discipline, stamina, strategy, and patient endurance.

Consequently, Scripture says, "Let us lay aside every weight, and the sin which so easily ensnares us, and let us run with endurance the race that is set before us" (v. 1). The phrase *let us* is used throughout Hebrews, challenging readers to apply the truths they have heard (cf. 4:1, 11, 14, 16; 6:1; 10:22–24). The phrase is a gracious way to exhort people to embrace what is being taught.

Believers are exhorted to do three things to run the race of faith:

(1) ***"Lay aside every weight"*** (v. 1). The word *weight* means "bulk" or "mass." It could refer to excess body weight; a heavy, bulky garment; or anything binding the runner's body and thus encumbering him. For Christians, it means ridding themselves of everything that retards their progress, even though some hindrances may not be sinful. In context, it refers to the Jewish traditions that hindered these believers from growing in their faith.

(2) *"Lay aside . . . the sin which so easily ensnares [besets] us"* (v. 1). The Greek word for "ensnares" is used only here in the New Testament and conveys the idea of sin encircling someone, impeding his progress. The definite article *the* preceding the word *sin* denotes a particular sin: that of believers returning to their Jewish roots. Today believers might apply the exhortation to a specific sin in their lives that needs to be discarded.

(3) *"Run with endurance the race that is set before us"* (v. 1). This race is not a sprint. It is a marathon that requires endurance to finish. Runners must shed all unnecessary weights, patiently pace themselves, and persistently endure as they faithfully struggle through life to the finish line.

Perfect Example

The greatest encouragement to persevering in faith is the supreme example of Jesus Christ:

> *Looking unto Jesus, the author and finisher of our faith, who for the joy that was set before Him endured the cross, despising the shame, and has sat down at the right hand of the throne of God* (v. 2).

The word *looking* means to turn one's eyes away from all distractions and fix them continually on one thing. In context, that means fixing one's eyes on Jesus. A runner must focus on the course and goal before him, not on his surroundings, or he will be distracted, lose his stride, slacken his pace, and even fall.

In the race of faith, the believer's ultimate example is not the witnesses in Hebrews 11, but Jesus, who is "the author and finisher of our faith." The word *author* connotes an originator, founder, or chief leader. Jesus is the "forerunner" (6:20) of the faith, setting the supreme, perfect example that all Christians are to follow. He is the greatest example of patient endurance under severe persecution, having been tried illegally and crucified (cf. Isa. 53:7; 1 Pet. 2:21–23). Jesus is also the "finisher" or "completer" of the believer's faith; through His death and resurrection, He secured eternal salvation for all who trust in Him (Heb. 5:9).

Jesus endured the cross "for the joy that was set before Him" (12:2). Clearly, His joy was not in being crucified. It was the most disgraceful and dehumanizing death known. Yet He did not allow the privation, suffering, contempt, and cursing to dissuade Him from God's will. He freely bore the shame and disgrace to provide for our salvation.

The "joy that was set before Him" was His final victory over Satan and sin, thus completing God's work of redemption, bringing glory to God the Father by implementing His plan of salvation, and being reunited with the Father in heaven.

After His postresurrection ministry, Jesus ascended to heaven from the Mount of Olives (Acts 1:8–10) and "sat down at the right hand of the throne of God" (Heb. 12:2: cf. 1:3; 8:1; 10:12). The word *sat* is in the Greek perfect tense, meaning that, at a point in time, Jesus took His seat on a throne at the Father's right hand and remains there, signifying the completion of His ministry. His seated position at the Father's right hand is a sign of triumph and foreshadows or portends His and all believers' future and final victory (cf. 1:13–14).

Personal Endurance

Scripture then commands readers to analyze Christ's suffering: "For consider Him who endured such hostility from sinners against Himself, lest you become weary and discouraged in your souls" (12:3).

The word *consider* (Greek, *analogizomai*) is our word *analogy* and means to reckon, add up, and weigh Christ's sufferings against our own. Ponder this: Jesus was born in a stable to poor parents who fled Jerusalem with

Him to save His life; He was reared in a deplorable city, lost His father early in life, and had no permanent home during His ministry. He was considered mentally unbalanced and demon-possessed; He was disbelieved by His family, hated and opposed by the religious leaders, forsaken by His disciples, tried illegally, and scourged and beaten before He was finally crucified.

Looking at His suffering would make theirs seem insignificant. Thus they "should not become weary and discouraged in [their] souls" (v. 3). The word *weary* means to become exhausted and possibly ill due to persecution. Some Jewish believers had grown weary, which led to discouragement. They had become fainthearted, lost confidence and enthusiasm, and had slackened in their commitment.

Then the text goes one step further in comparing the Jewish believers' suffering to that of Jesus: "You have not yet resisted to bloodshed, striving against sin" (v. 4). "You" refers to believers who had previously faced persecution at the hands of their brethren (10:32–34). They had suffered physically and materially; but none had endured the suffering Jesus had, nor had anyone given his life for the gospel. These believers needed to ponder afresh the Messiah's suffering and renew their commitment to Him, thus gaining strength to persevere in the race of faith.

They were still "striving against sin" (12:4). The word *strive* means to contend, as in a race, or to engage in conflict, as in a boxing match. Their conflict required them to stand against sinful men wanting to harm them as they harmed Jesus and against the sin of renouncing their faith in Christ by returning to their Jewish roots.

In our race of faith, we must heed the admonishment to consider all Jesus faced as the Originator and Completer of our faith. We, too, must remain faithful and not become weary or discouraged but persevere patiently, with endurance, to the finish line.

CHAPTER 26

THE LORD'S CHASTENING
Hebrews 12:5–17

Tribulation and suffering befall all true Christians sometime in their lives. The believers addressed in the book of Hebrews were no exception. Persecution had left them weary in soul and emotionally drained. They had suffered severely and had experienced extreme privation and loss.

In Hebrews God reminds us all that our relationship to Him is as sons to a father, and whatever chastening our heavenly Father allows us to face is for our good and ultimate righteousness. God is never responsible for the evil that wicked people do, but He allows it as an instrument to discipline His children. Chastening and suffering bring believers to maturity in Christ.

Hebrews 12:5–17 explains the Lord's chastening and what it should accomplish.

Remembering It

The book of Hebrews was written to Jewish believers in Christ. What better way to begin this section than by reminding them of God's chastening in the Old Testament:

> *And you have forgotten the exhortation which speaks to you as to sons: "My son, do not despise the chastening [discipline] of the Lord, nor be discouraged when you are rebuked by Him; for whom the Lord loves He chastens, and scourges every son whom He receives"* (Heb. 12:5–6; cf. Prov. 3:11–12).

The Lord calls those He addresses "sons" (Greek, *huios*), indicating He considers them true believers. They were adopted into His family through faith in Christ. The word *chastening* (Greek, *paideia*) is used in the context of parents lovingly disciplining their children through training and education. *Paideia* was never used to speak of punishment. It connotes instruction in what is good and right, such as instilling virtue and instituting proper correction to guard a child from doing evil. *Scourge* actually means to flog with a whip and is used figuratively for the Lord's corrective discipline, comparing Him to a father who uses a switch to correct his child's behavior.

Discipline confirms God's love and proves the person being corrected truly belongs to Him. Even Jesus Christ, God's Son, was made perfect through what He suffered (Heb. 2:10). So the Lord's chastening is positive, not negative, to bring encouragement, not discouragement.

One should not "despise" (12:5) or look with aversion or contempt on the Lord's chastening. Discipline does not happen by chance but is the perfect will of God the Father, out of necessity. Remember, God never punishes His children for their iniquities because all their punishment was borne by Jesus Christ on the cross (Rom. 8:11).

Receiving It

Chastening is to be received as correction from God:

> *If you endure chastening [discipline], God deals with you as with sons; for what son is there whom a father does not chasten? But if you are without chastening, of which all have become partakers, then you are illegitimate and not sons* (Heb. 12:7–8).

Older English versions begin verse 7 with "if"; but a better translation of the Greek text is "for," indicating God allows the persecution believers face for chastening purposes. Remember, chastening is not punishment but, rather, part of God's training and education to curb and correct misdirection or evil in a believer's life (cf. Dt. 8:5; 2 Sam. 7:14). We are to endure or remain under God's discipline because, over time, it will bring us to spiritual maturity. God's discipline is a sign to believers that they are God's children. People who receive no discipline are illegitimate, that is, not true believers.

An illustration is how human fathers train their sons:

> *Furthermore, we have had human fathers who corrected us, and we paid them respect. Shall we not much more readily be in subjection to the Father of spirits and live? For they indeed for a few days chastened us as seemed best to them, but He for our profit, that we may be partakers of His holiness* (Heb. 12:9–10).

If we respect and revere our fallible human fathers who chasten us, how much more should we respect our divine Father, who is infallible? He is the Father of our spiritual and physical lives. He not only has our eternal well-being in mind but all that is involved in our present existence. He knows exactly how much and what type of discipline we need and can handle (cf. 1 Cor. 10:13).

An earthly father only chastens "for a few days" (Heb. 12:10), until the child is grown. He metes out the discipline in a manner he deems correct and wise; but he may use the wrong method out of frustration or anger, discouraging the child who then turns away from him with bitterness and resentment.

However, our divine Father has perfect knowledge and always disciplines His children wisely, correctly, and profitably. His goal is to make them "partakers of His holiness" (v. 10).

Discipline, whether from God or man, never "seems to be joyful for the present, but painful; nevertheless, afterward it yields the peaceable fruit of righteousness to those who have been trained by it" (v. 11). No matter how severe, discipline will produce peace and righteousness. Thus believers should regard the experience with joy, knowing it will strengthen their spiritual lives and deepen their relationships with God (cf. Jas. 1:2–4).

Jesus clearly taught that all believers must be pruned and purified to have fruitful lives (Jn. 15:2).

Responding to It

Since chastening is inevitable, the author used the word *therefore* to call on believers to respond positively to the experience. Quoting from Isaiah 35:3, he said, "Therefore strengthen the hands which hang down, and the feeble knees, and make straight paths for your feet, so that what is lame may not be dislocated, but rather be healed" (Heb. 12:12–13).

The verses describe someone about to collapse physically, spiritually, and emotionally from the chastening; and they exhort the individual not to faint from exhaustion under it. He is to make sure his feet stay on the "straight paths" because if he veers off onto a rough, bumpy path in his fatigued state, he could easily dislocate (turn or twist out of joint) his leg or foot, disqualifying him from the race.

In other words, the spiritually weak Jewish believers who were being persecuted were ready to return to their Jewish roots and needed an inner resolve to stay the course in their new faith. If they stayed the course, remained under God's discipline with a correct attitude, and looked to Him for strength to endure the persecution, He would heal them and bring them through victoriously.

Then the author admonished them, "Pursue peace with all people, and holiness, without which no one will see the Lord: looking carefully lest anyone fall short of the grace of God; lest any root of bitterness springing up cause trouble, and by this many become defiled" (vv. 14–15).

The word *pursue* means to try eagerly and earnestly to seek "peace" and "holiness" with "all people," whether Christians or those who persecute them. The word *holiness* involves the believer's sanctification in two ways: positional and progressive. Christians possess positional sanctification before God immediately upon receiving Christ as Savior. Yet they are being progressively sanctified through daily obedience to God's commands. People who earnestly seek peace and holiness demonstrate they are true believers and, as such, "will see the Lord."

The author warns Christians regarding their responsibility for the spiritual welfare of their fellow believers. They are to be "looking carefully" (see or give oversight, v. 15) with due diligence over their spiritual lives and attitudes toward others within the congregation for three reasons:

(1) *"Lest anyone fall short of the grace of God"* (v. 15). Some interpret the phrase to refer to a person who professes faith in Christ but falls short of salvation because of persecution. In context, the phrase refers to believers who fail to appreciate and appropriate God's grace, especially during persecution. Failing to do so makes Christ inoperative in one's spiritual walk and can result in falling from grace (cf. Gal. 5:4) or being severed from the blessings and fellowship of the indwelling Holy Spirit.

(2) *"Lest any root of bitterness springing up cause trouble, and by this many become defiled"* (Heb. 12:15). Failing to appropriate God's grace during persecution and suffering can lead to bitterness that will be manifested through actions and words. Bitterness eventually poisons the congregation; and "many become defiled," often causing major divisions and schisms. The phrase is quoted from Deuteronomy 29:18 to illustrate how bitterness corrupted Israel in the wilderness and led to discouragement and idolatry.

(3) *"Lest there be any fornicator or profane person like Esau, who for one morsel of food sold his birthright"* (Heb. 12:16; cf. Gen. 25:27–34). Esau is singled out to drive home the point. Scripture never calls Esau a "fornicator" (sexually immoral), although he probably was because of his involvement with heathen women. The word can be taken metaphorically, describing him as "profane" (unholy, irreligious, godless), having no regard for spiritual things and viewing them with contempt.

Esau was in line to inherit the birthright and attendant blessings; but being a secular man, he cared nothing about such things or his privileges from God. Instead, he trampled them underfoot. He sold his birthright for a "morsel of food," a paltry price for a priceless treasure. Though he forfeited his birthright and blessing, his sonship remained.

After seeing his error, Esau wanted the birthright and blessing back; but "he was rejected, for he found no place [opportunity] for repentance [a change of mind], though he sought it diligently with tears" (Heb. 12:17). Esau was rejected because his decision was irrevocable.

The illustration of Esau's willingness to forfeit his birthright and blessing sent a pointed and chilling message to Jewish believers. Their birthright was provided at Christ's expense through His sacrifice on the cross. To return to their Jewish roots would forever cut them off from blessing and, ultimately, from maturity in Christ.

As believers, we must persevere through chastening and persecution because, in the end, God will bless us and bring us to maturity in Jesus.

CHAPTER 27

THE FINAL WARNING
Hebrews 12:18–29

In a fifth and final warning to Jewish believers in Christ, the book of Hebrews contrasts the experience of God's people at Mount Sinai as they received the Mosaic Covenant with the blessedness of being associated with Mount Zion under the New Covenant. Both Mounts represent defining moments as God spoke to His people. For Israel, Mount Sinai was a place of terror and judgment should the nation disobey God's Law. However, Mount Zion is pictured as a place of grace, joy, and eternal redemption for all believers in Christ.

Hebrews 12:18–29 summarizes the main thrust of the book, emphasizing that what Christians possess in Christ, their great High Priest, puts them in a far better position than under the Mosaic Covenant.

The Mount of Dread

To make an indelible impression on his readers, the author provided a soul-stirring description of what their Jewish forefathers experienced at Mount Sinai:

> *For you have not come to the mountain that may be touched and that burned with fire, and to blackness and darkness and tempest, and the sound of a trumpet and the voice of words, so that those who heard it begged that the word should not be spoken to them anymore. (For they could not endure what was commanded: "And if so much as a beast touches the mountain, it shall be stoned or shot*

with an arrow." And so terrifying was the sight that Moses said,
"I am exceedingly afraid and trembling") (vv. 18–21; cf. Ex.
19:10–25; 20:18–21; Dt. 4:10–24).

Moses told the Israelites to wash their clothes and refrain from sexual relations with their wives for two days; and on the third day, God would speak to them from Mount Sinai. The mountain was off limits to both people and animals. Anyone touching even its base was to be "stoned or shot with an arrow" (Heb. 12:20).

On the third day, a thick cloud of smoke completely engulfed Mount Sinai. Thunder and lightning filled the atmosphere as a violent earthquake shook the mountain. Darkness descended, and the Israelites trembled at the eerie feeling of doom.

God instructed Moses to lead Israel out of its camp to meet with Him at Mount Sinai. A loud, deafening trumpet was sounded, whereupon the Lord descended from heaven to the top of the mountain. The visible manifestation overwhelmed Israel with wonderment and awe. When the people heard God speak, they stood petrified, trembling in fear; and they begged Moses to speak instead of God: "You speak with us, and we will hear; but let not God speak with us, lest we die" (Ex. 20:19).

Hebrews 12:19–20 explains they were convinced that if God continued speaking His Law, they would perish because of their sin. Initially, even Moses was frightened: "I am exceedingly afraid and trembling" (v. 21).

At Sinai, Israel stood before a holy, omnipotent, omniscient God who was unapproachable by vile, sinful man. Mount Sinai represented the Old Covenant, with its Mosaic system of laws that required people to keep all its commandments—which was humanly impossible. Those who broke the Law were subject to judgment, separation from God, and eventual death and punishment.

God originated the sacrificial system to provide atonement for sin so that sinful people could approach a holy God. Yet these sacrifices could never take away sin (10:4); they merely functioned as a vicarious substitute to propitiate the wrath of God's judgment against them.

The Mount of Deliverance

A contrast is made between the terrors experienced at Mount Sinai and the blessings believers possess in their relationship to Jesus Christ.

First, Mount Zion is in heaven, not on Earth: "But you have come to Mount Zion and to the city of the living God, the heavenly Jerusalem" (12:22). This city is free from bondage (Gal. 4:26), was sought by Abraham (Heb. 11:10), and is described in the book of Revelation (Rev. 21:2—22:5). It is God's abode and a place of rich blessing and joy where believers will dwell with Jesus Christ.

Second, someday believers in Christ will be in the presence of "an innumerable company of angels" who are gathered in festive celebration (Heb. 12:22; cf. Rev. 5:11). These angels continually worship God and stand ready to carry out His will in heaven and on Earth. In the New Jerusalem, we will worship and serve alongside them.

The words *general assembly* (Greek, *panegurei*; Heb. 12:23) refer to large, festive gatherings, such as the Olympics. Scholars differ on whether to connect them with the word *angels* (v. 22), *church* (v. 23), or both. Most commentators connect the words with *angels* and translate the phrase "to myriads of angels in festal gathering."

Third, Mount Zion is the eternal home for Christians, referred to as the "church of the firstborn who are registered in heaven" (v. 23). The word *church* (Greek, *ekklesia*) refers to a "called out group of people" comprised of regenerated Jews and Gentiles who, from the day of Pentecost to the Rapture, constitute the body of Christ. The church also is referred to as "firstborn," identifying its spiritual birthright in union with Christ as Savior and making believers "heirs of God and joint heirs with Christ" (Rom. 8:17).

Today the church dwells on Earth, but its citizenship already has been "registered in heaven" (Heb. 12:23; cf. Lk. 10:20; Rev. 13:8; 21:27); and it will one day reside in the heavenly Jerusalem. This will be a festive gathering of the church in heaven, in contrast to the terrifying setting of Sinai.

Fourth, the supreme Ruler in heaven is "God the Judge of all" (Heb. 12:23). This verse emphasizes His position and supreme right to judge all things in heaven and on Earth. Israelites at Mount Sinai could not approach God's presence; they would have died. However, at Christ's crucifixion, the veil into the Temple's Holy of Holies was torn from top to bottom (Mt. 27:51), giving all believers access to God's presence, where they can receive mercy and grace (Heb. 4:16). That was an enlightening thought to someone ready to forsake Christ, return to ritualistic Judaism, and suffer God's judgment because of his decision.

Fifth, the phrase *to the spirits of just men made perfect* (12:23) refers to Old Testament saints whose spirits and souls are in heaven without their resurrected bodies. They are "just" (justified), or redeemed, and need to be "made perfect" (complete) in their redemption—which will occur when they receive their resurrected bodies prior to Christ's Second Coming (Dan. 12:2; Heb. 11:40).

Sixth, all come to faith through "Jesus the Mediator of the new covenant" (12:24). The word *new* (Greek, *neos*) refers to new in time and emphasizes the revelation that Jesus is the Mediator of the New Covenant through His shed blood, which provides complete cleansing from sin (8:7–13; 9:11–15; 10:15–18).

Seventh, Christ "sprinkling" His blood on the cross "speaks better things than that of Abel" (12:24). After Abel was murdered by his brother Cain, his blood cried out to God from the ground for judgment (Gen. 4:10). However, Christ's shed blood is far better because it purchased salvation and cleanses all believers from sin.

The choice between being under the Old Covenant of Law or the New Covenant of grace could not be clearer: Mount Zion is light, grace, peace, rest, forgiveness of sin, inexpressible joy, access to God, and eternal life. Mount Sinai is fear, death, and judgment. Believers must choose Mount Zion.

The Moment of Decision

God has another warning to anyone considering deserting the faith:

> *See that you do not refuse Him who speaks. For if they did not escape who refused Him who spoke on earth, much more shall we not escape if we turn away from Him who speaks from heaven, whose voice then shook the earth; but now He has promised, saying, "Yet once more I shake not only the earth, but also heaven"* (Heb. 12:25–26).

God warns believers that if Israel did not escape temporal judgment on Earth when it refused to heed God who spoke to them at Mount Sinai, they certainly will not escape God's temporal discipline if they refuse to heed His message from heaven through Christ. Greater is their responsibility to the message of God in Christ (cf. 2:2–3).

When God spoke at Mount Sinai, "[His] voice . . . shook the earth." It was symbolic of a great shaking in the future when He will shake "not only the earth, but also heaven" (12:26). The verse quotes Haggai 2:6 and refers to the shaking before and at Christ's Second Coming (cf. Joel 3:16; Zech. 14:4–5; Mt. 24:29; Rev. 16:18, 20) when He will destroy Gentile world rule (Dan. 2:34–35, 44–45; Hag. 2:21–22).

The author mentioned a "removal of those things that are being shaken, as of things that are made, that the things which cannot be shaken may remain" (Heb. 12:27). The destructible things are those under the Mosaic Covenant; the permanent things are the New Covenant blessings in Christ, the New Jerusalem, and all that pertains to God's eternal Kingdom. A final shaking will take place after the Millennial Kingdom, when God destroys the material universe (2 Pet. 3:10, 12; Rev. 20:11) and creates a new heaven and new Earth that will be eternal

(2 Pet. 3:13; Rev. 21:1).

An application to the entire warning follows: "Therefore, since we are receiving a kingdom which cannot be shaken, let us have grace [be grateful], by which we may serve God acceptably with reverence and godly fear" (Heb. 12:28). Since God has provided grace, salvation in Christ, and future blessings in an eternal Kingdom, these persecuted Jewish believers to whom the book of Hebrews is addressed should in no way consider returning to Judaism. Instead, they should serve God gratefully, with prayer and praise, and worship Him in reverence and awe. Their faithful perseverance would determine their rewards in the Kingdom (1 Cor. 3:14).

There is a final, poignant warning: "For our God is a consuming fire" (Heb. 12:29; cf. Dt. 4:24). All who returned to Judaism would face God's displeasure and discipline. True, God bestows grace on all believers. But He is also a God of judgment and will discipline us as He did Israel in the wilderness and Esau, mentioned earlier (Heb. 12:16–17).

CHAPTER 28

THE CHRISTIAN'S COMMITMENT
Hebrews 13:1–6

To this point, the book of Hebrews has stressed the superiority of Christ, while exhorting believers not to leave the church because of persecution but to go on to Christian maturity.

In chapter 13, Hebrews abruptly shifts to moral and ethical issues of the Christian life and exhorts believers to walk their talk: What you claim to believe about God should be evident in your daily relationships with believers and nonbelievers alike. Warren Wiersbe said it well: "There is no division between doctrine and duty, revelation and responsibility. The two always go together."[1]

The first six verses of chapter 13 contain moral exhortations concerning living the Christian faith. Since no connectives link to the preceding material, each exhortation stands on its own as an individual command.

Compassion

First, believers are to show fellow Christians love: "Let brotherly love continue" (13:1). This command acknowledges that such love existed among these Christians, and it admonished them not to let it grow cold. The Greek word for "brotherly love," *philadelphia*, refers to showing affection and fondness for fellow believers by offering them kindness and sympathy and helping to meet their needs. Such love binds the body of Christ together in an unbreakable union of deep, heartfelt affection that is nurtured over time and prompts believers to look after one another:

The word "brother" in the Greek, adelphos, *means "from the same womb." Thus, the basis of their Christian fondness and affection for each other, the source of their Christian fellowship, was the fact that they all came from the same source, having one Father, God.*[2]

Christians are commanded to continue showing this type of love. Love is foundational to everything in the family and fellowship of the church (cf. Jn. 13:34–35; 1 Cor. 13; 1 Th. 4:9; 1 Jn. 3:14; Rev. 2:1–7). Love was present, but persecution was causing it to wane (cf. Rev. 2:1–7). The exhortation spoke to those who had grown cold and indifferent to their Christian brethren and were considering leaving the church and returning to Judaism.

When love within the church starts to disappear, the fellowship weakens. This command to love is an ever-needful reminder to the church, especially with the schisms and splits erupting within many churches today.

Second, Scripture says, "Do not forget to entertain strangers, for by so doing some have unwittingly entertained angels" (Heb. 13:2). The word *entertain* (Greek, *philoxenia*) is better translated "love of strangers." Though it connotes showing love to all people and receiving them with fraternal friendliness, it especially entails loving the brethren by opening one's heart and home and providing resources to help when needed.

Hospitality was essential in the first century, especially for the believers. Due to persecution, many had fled their homes, leaving everything behind to become wanderers until they found a place to resettle. The local inns in the unfamiliar and faraway places were limited, expensive, often rowdy, and sometimes abusive and hostile to strangers—not places where Christians would feel comfortable. Such "strangers" were in great need of Christian hospitality.

Lodging travelers (especially preachers) was an expected, needful, and common practice. These brethren needed safety, shelter, and food for themselves and their animals, as well as information or help. Bishops and church leaders were expected to show hospitality (1 Tim. 3:2; Ti. 1:8). Godly women were praised for lodging strangers (1 Tim. 5:10).

This command is couched in language that suggests some Christians were refusing to welcome strangers. The apostle Peter commanded that hospitality be shown "to one another without grumbling" (1 Pet. 4:9). The apostle John praised Gaius for how he received strangers (3 Jn. 5–8). There is one exception: Christians are explicitly told not to greet or receive into their home false teachers who do not abide in the doctrine of Christ (2 Jn. 9–11).

Some who welcomed strangers did not know they were entertaining angels (Heb. 13:2). This text gives no specific example, but the Old Testament provides a number of illustrations where God's people entertained angels. For example, Abraham (Gen. 18:1–8) and Lot (19:1–3) entertained the angels who came to announce Sodom and Gomorrah's destruction. Gideon entertained the Angel of the Lord when he was commissioned to deliver Israel from the Midianites (Jud. 6:11–24). Zorah, Manoah's husband, entertained the Angel of the Lord when He came to announce that his wife would give birth to Samson (13:3–20). We should never expect to entertain angels, but it may sometimes happen; and we never know how doing so will impact our lives. Jesus revealed that ministering to strangers, especially His Jewish brethren, was the same as ministering to Him (Mt. 25:35–40).

Third, we are to remember to sympathize with suffering saints: "Remember the prisoners as if chained with them—those who are mistreated—since you yourselves are in the body also" (Heb. 13:3). This verse refers to believers incarcerated and suffering physically and mentally because they confessed Christ as Savior. Many would be crucified, burned at the stake, killed in the Roman arena, or impaled on stakes and set on fire to become living torches at Emperor Nero's garden parties.

Those not imprisoned were told to view themselves as suffering along with their brethren "as if chained with them" because of their bonds through faith in Christ. Though free, they, too, could someday be subject to the same inhumane fate. So Christians should see themselves as being imprisoned with their fellow believers, as if their own bodies were receiving the same treatment (cf. 1 Cor. 12:26; Gal. 6:2; Col. 4:18). This was a sober exhortation to motivate Christians to sympathize with their suffering brethren.

Chasteness

Couples are commanded to practice sexual sanctity in marriage: "Marriage is honorable among all, and the bed undefiled; but fornicators and adulterers God will judge" (Heb. 13:4). A better translation is, "Let marriage by all be respected, and let the marriage bed be undefiled, for the sexually immoral and adulterers God will judge." This is an exhortation to honor marriage as precious and highly esteemed.

Scripture cites two abuses to marriage: (1) false teachers who forbid Christians to marry (1 Tim. 4:3) and (2) fornication and adultery. The word *bed* (Greek, *koite*) is used of a married couple and emphasizes keeping the sexual relationship pure. The word *undefiled* refers to any moral impurity, uncleanness, or defilement. In context, it refers to adultery and sexual immorality; that is, refraining from "fornication" (Greek, *pornoi*), sexual immorality, or adultery. Fornication dishonors a marriage before it takes place, and adultery defiles and dishonors a marriage after it is consummated. "God will judge" and condemn such actions, even if society accepts and condones them.

Contentment

Christians are to be satisfied with their material state in life:

Let your conduct [manner of life] be without covetousness [i.e., love of money]; be content with such things as you have. For He Himself has said, "I will never leave you nor forsake you." So we may boldly say: "The LORD is my helper; I will not fear. What can man do to me?" (Heb. 13:5–6).

This passage issues a strong warning against loving money. Believers are commanded to be content with what they have, no matter what their state in life. Most likely, persecution and deprivation had caused some to grumble and covet (cf. 10:32–34).

Covetousness is defined as an inordinate desire or craving for wealth and possessions or the greedy desire to acquire the possessions of another. Scripture is full of illustrations on how greed and covetousness caused men to compromise their commitments to God (Achan, Josh. 7:1, 5, 26; Gehazi, 2 Ki. 5:15–27; Ananias and Sapphira, Acts 5:1–10). Scripture condemns covetousness and the love of money and continually warns Christians to guard against such cravings (cf. Mt. 6:24; 1 Tim. 6:8–10).

Believers today live in a materialistic society and can easily succumb to the belief that wealth and possessions produce inner peace and lasting satisfaction. However, the apostle Paul said Christians should be content with their situations, and God will supply all they need according to His riches in glory through Christ (Phil. 4:12, 19).

Two great encouragements are given to believers, both quotations from the Old Testament. First, "For He Himself [God the Father] has said, 'I will never leave you nor forsake you'" (Heb. 13:5). This promise is stated twice in the Old Testament: once to Israel and Joshua when Moses commissioned Joshua to lead the nation into the Land of Promise (Dt. 31:6, 8) and again when King David commissioned his son Solomon to build the Temple (1 Chr. 28:20).

Security is not found in money or material possessions, but rather in God's personal promise and faithfulness never to fail or forsake believers under any condition. The Lord will never abandon, desert, or leave you alone if you belong to Him.

Second, because of God's faithfulness, "We may boldly say: 'The LORD is my helper; I will not fear. What can man do to me?'" (Heb. 13:6; quoted from the Septuagint translation of Psalm 118:6). The word *we* links the author with his readers and expresses bold confidence in God meeting their needs.

Believers should have bold confidence because the Lord is with us to help us in every circumstance. We should have no fear because God is our Helper; man can do nothing to us unless God allows it. Knowing all these things, Christians should face life's challenges with confidence and courage and trust in God's help.

Endnotes

[1] Warren W. Wiersbe, *The Wiersbe Bible Commentary: New Testament*, 2nd ed. (Colorado Springs, CO: David C. Cook, 2007), 842. Previously published as *The Bible Exposition Commentary* (Wheaton, IL: Victor Books, 1989).

[2] Kenneth S. Wuest, "Heb. 12:28—13:2," *Wuest's Word Studies From the Greek New Testament* (Grand Rapids, MI: Eerdmans, 1997), Logos Bible Software edition.

CHAPTER 29

COUNSELING THE CHRISTIAN
Hebrews 13:7–17

Chapter 13 of Hebrews contains the book's final admonishment. Whereas verses 1–6 provide practical and personal exhortation on how believers should live in Christ, verses 7–17 focus more on theological issues and the gospel.

The Believer's Consistency

Verse 7 exhorts readers to recall the ministries and conduct of their past leaders: "Remember those who rule over [lead] you, who have spoken the word of God to you, whose faith follow, considering the outcome of their conduct."

The word *remember* tells readers to be mindful continually of leaders now with the Lord, whose lives and preaching influenced them and laid the foundation of their commitment. Those faithful leaders exemplified true faith and did not waver in their consistency or devotion to Christ. Readers are to keep recalling the messages they heard and carefully imitate the faith of these departed saints.

Leaders come and go; eventually they die and are often forgotten. But one Leader never changes and is with us always. He is Jesus Christ, "the same yesterday, today, and forever" (v. 8). This profound, succinct summary about Jesus Christ affirms that He will never be superseded. No need to fear that Christ or His message of salvation will ever change—not now or in the future.

Christ is the same "yesterday." He is the changeless, eternal, immutable Son of God in His person, office, and teaching. He is the same "today." What He was yesterday is true of Him now. God has not changed Christ's original message or the gospel preached to these believers. Jesus, who was so real to them at the inception of their salvation, remains the same. And Christ is the same "forever." What He was yesterday and today, He will be throughout eternity.

Consequently, Scripture commands believers to guard against false doctrines and practices: "Do not be carried about with various [i.e. diverse] and strange doctrines. For it is good that the heart be established by grace, not with foods which have not profited those who have been occupied with them" (v. 9).

They were to guard against a variety of doctrines and practices that differed from what they had been taught. Though the "strange doctrines" are not specified, they probably involved traditional Jewish beliefs taught by Pharisees, scribes, and elders who embellished the Law of Moses with their own oral traditions (cf. Mk. 7:1–9). Such teaching would contradict the gospel of grace and their new Christian faith.

Many believers probably focused on the Jewish laws and regulations relating to foods associated with Jewish ceremonial observances. These dietary laws (some biblical but many manmade) are of no spiritual profit in the Christian life. In fact, they are foreign to the grace of God and gospel of Christ. So the Scriptures warn against practices that would elevate Judaism over Christianity. In the past, these believers had blindly followed such rituals and ceremonies, which profited them nothing for salvation.

God reminds the readers, "The heart [is] established by [God's] grace" (Heb. 13:9). God's grace is communicated through the hearts of believers. If the heart is not purged from evil and made stable in the Lord, the believer cannot draw near to God. Instead, he or she will be influenced by strange and useless teachings and will not experience the internal working of God's grace that is necessary to bring a Christian to spiritual maturity.

The Believer's Commitment

The author is specific in telling Jewish believers that, if they continue to embrace the Levitical system, they have no part in the New Covenant blessings:

> *We have an altar from which those who serve the tabernacle have no right to eat* (v. 10).

Commentators differ widely concerning the word *altar* (v. 10). Some believe it refers to the heavenly sanctuary; others say it refers to the cross (place of Christ's sacrifice) or Christ Himself or the Lord's Supper or Christ's sacrificial death. It would seem best to view the word as referring to the whole sacrificial death and atoning work of Christ, as contrasted to the altar where Levitical sacrifices were offered in the Tabernacle.

In other words, Jewish believers had the altar in Christ. Those who still went to the Temple to practice Levitical sacrifice were told to stop doing so and trust in Jesus as the once-for-all sacrifice to take away their sin. Bringing animal sacrifices through the Levitical system indicated a failure to trust Christ's sacrifice.

Those who practiced the Levitical system were not availing themselves of the benefits that Christ's atoning work provided.

Priests who served in the Tabernacle had the right to eat the sin offerings (Lev. 4:22–35; 6:25–26), with one exception: on the Day of Atonement (16:27). That sin offering they had "no right to eat" (Heb. 13:10): "The bodies of those animals, whose blood is brought into the sanctuary [the Holy of Holies] by the high priest for sin, are burned outside the camp" (v. 11; cf. Lev. 16:27). Of this sin offering, neither the high priest nor people could partake.

The burning of sacrifices "outside the camp" on the Day of Atonement (Yom Kippur) is applied to Christ's similar experience of suffering outside Jerusalem. "Therefore Jesus also, that He might sanctify the people with His own blood, suffered outside the gate" (Heb. 13:12). Disposal of the Day of Atonement sacrifice outside the "gate" (Jerusalem) foreshadowed Jesus' atoning work. His crucifixion between two thieves (outside Jerusalem) was the worst shame, disgrace, condemnation, and repudiation that could have been inflicted on Him at the time of His death.

The phrase *that He might sanctify [set apart] the people* (v. 12) refers to both the purpose and people in relationship to Jesus' death. The purpose was to remove the sin and guilt of those who received Christ and set them apart to be His holy people. "The people" who received Christ as Savior were continually to be setting themselves apart from the sins of this world system and their past lives in Judaism.

On the basis of their faith in Christ, Scripture says, "Therefore let us go forth to Him, outside the camp, bearing His reproach" (v. 13). That is, go "outside the camp" of Judaism and identify with Christ, who was rejected by the Jewish leaders.

These people were at a crossroads: Would they return to Judaism or identify with Jesus, even when doing so meant suffering "reproach" (rejection, alienation, scorn, and disgrace) as outcasts from their families, religion, and communities?

They were reminded, "Here we have no continuing city, but we seek the one to come" (v. 14). Like Abraham, believers are pilgrims who have no permanent dwelling place on Earth. Our eyes are not to be fixed on an earthly city and world system, but on a heavenly, eternal one—the New Jerusalem, whose Architect and Maker is God (11:10, 16; 12:22; Rev. 21:1—22:5). Christ's followers are not to seek temporary, worldly gratification, but to keep their eyes on the eternal and spiritual qualities found in Christ.

The Believer's Consecration

The final counsel appears in the last three verses. First, offer the sacrifice of praise: "Therefore by Him let us continually offer the sacrifice of praise to God, that is, the fruit of our lips, giving thanks to

His name" (Heb. 13:15). Did God require sacrifices from Jewish believers in Christ? Yes! Not the sacrifices of slain animals, but the "sacrifice of praise" and thanksgiving that comes from an appreciative heart for all He has provided in salvation through Christ. A truly thankful person continually worships God with praise.

Second, share: "But do not forget to do good and to share [fellowship], for with such sacrifices God is well pleased" (v. 16). Believers are to do good deeds for those within the church. These actions can include encouraging others or sharing financial and material resources to help Christian brothers and sisters in need (1 Jn. 3:17).

Third, be in subjection to spiritual leaders. Earlier the author told readers to submit to past spiritual leaders; here he referred to current leaders. God has placed shepherds within the church to watch over the sheep and guard them from false doctrines. A Christian is to "obey . . . and be submissive" (Heb. 13:17) by yielding to these spiritual leaders as long as they are true to Christ's teachings, because they "watch out for [their] souls." The word *watch* means always being awake and alert to the needs of those in the church. The leaders are shepherds whose responsibility it is to care for the deep needs of the flock, especially the feeble and fainthearted. Such leaders have a serious stewardship of oversight and will be required to "give account" of their leadership responsibilities before the Judgment Seat of Christ (v. 17).

The phrase *let them do so with joy and not with grief, for that would be unprofitable for you* is not addressed to the leaders, but to the people (v. 17). Christians are not to be self-willed, stiff-necked, opinionated, selfish, or stubborn when it comes to being led. They are to submit willingly to pastors, elders, and deacons so that these people can lead with "joy." Being unsubmissive causes church leaders "grief" and much difficulty in carrying out their stewardships. The result will be "unprofitable" to other Christians because they, too, will have no joy.

Rebellion against church leaders brings grief within the church and loss of reward at the Judgment Seat of Christ. In addition, a person's rebellion could intimate to the church leadership that the individual is not a believer and, without change, is destined for eternal punishment.

There is much wise counsel in this section of Hebrews. Let us examine our own lives and heed the advice given from God's Word.

CHAPTER 30

A FINAL EXHORTATION
Hebrews 13:18–25

The final eight verses of Hebrews 13 conclude the Epistle. In them, the author exhorted Jewish believers one last time through a beautiful prayer he offered on their behalf.

He promised to visit them soon and possibly bring Timothy with him. Meanwhile, he greeted the readers and their spiritual leaders, who were selected to shepherd, strengthen, and encourage the believers to submit to the Lord, who cares for their souls.

The exhortation focuses on Christ's shed blood, His resurrection, and the New Covenant, while telling believers to persevere to spiritual maturity. The final verses ask them to "bear with" (listen seriously and willingly to) the words of the letter.

A Final Prayer

First, the author requested prayer for himself and those with him:

> *Pray for us; for we are confident that we have a good conscience, in all things desiring to live honorably. But I especially urge you to do this, that I may be restored to you the sooner* (Heb. 13:18–19).

His request is encouraging and reveals his humility, as well as his need of and confidence in prayer. He did not view himself as superior to others less mature than he in the faith. He was "confident" that he and those with him had "good" (clear) consciences in their motives and actions and that they ministered in the will of God.

The author's ongoing desire was to live and minister honorably, with integrity before all men, but especially before the Jewish believers to whom he was writing. Prayer was all the more needful during his absence from them. The text implies something prohibited him from reuniting with his readers, but it is not specified.

He began his benediction by praying for his readers:

> *Now may the God of peace who brought up our Lord Jesus from the dead, that great Shepherd of the sheep, through the blood of the everlasting covenant, make you complete in every good work to do His will, working in you what is well pleasing in His sight, through Jesus Christ, to whom be glory forever and ever. Amen* (vv. 20–21).

Many fascinating elements here provide a beautiful message. First is the peace of God (v. 20). The focus is on peace secured through God the Father raising Jesus from the dead—not on any supposed discord between the author and those he addressed in the epistle, as some believe. It is through faith in Jesus Christ and God's grace that people are justified and receive peace with and from God (cf. Rom. 5:1–2).

Second, the power comes through God, "who brought up our Lord Jesus from the dead" (Heb. 13:20). This is the first explicit mention of Jesus' resurrection in the book of Hebrews, although it is assumed throughout the epistle. Christ's substitutionary sacrifice for us provided God's power and peace, as God declared when He raised Christ from the dead.

Third, Jesus is the preeminent Shepherd, "that great Shepherd of the sheep" (v. 20). The spiritual shepherds within the church care for the souls of the sheep; but over them is Jesus Christ, who oversees the path, provision, and protection of believers.

Fourth, the price paid for our salvation was "the blood of the everlasting covenant" (v. 20). Christ's blood was efficacious for the remission of humanity's sins. It paid the price for the penalty of sin and brings believers into a New Covenant relationship with God (Mt. 26:28;

cf. Heb. 8:6–13; 9:15—10:18). This covenant is called "everlasting" since it provides eternal life and cannot be annulled, abrogated, or replaced.

Fifth, the author prayed believers would be prepared for service, made "complete in every good work to do His will" (13:21). The word *complete* means "equipped" for whatever service the Lord calls someone to do. God is able to work through equipped believers to accomplish His will.

Sixth, all believers should strive to please God. This goal is accomplished by allowing Him to work in us "what is well pleasing in His sight" (v. 21). To have such a life, Christians must not serve the Lord through the work of the flesh, but rather by yielding complete control of their lives to the indwelling and filling of the Holy Spirit.

The prayer concludes with a doxology of praise "through Jesus Christ, to whom be glory forever and ever. Amen" (v. 21). The doxology can be addressed to God the Father, who is the subject of the prayer; Jesus Christ, the nearest antecedent within the prayer; or both. Praise and glory are attributed to God the Father and Jesus Christ, who provided the salvation mentioned in this prayer—but especially to Jesus, who provided reconciliation in the plan of salvation. This praise is to ascend to God "forever and ever." The benediction concludes the epistle's message, but not the epistle.

A Final Pronouncement

Verse 22 makes a final appeal to listen patiently to one more word of exhortation: "And I appeal to you, brethren, bear with the word of exhortation, for I have written to you in few words." The author spoke affectionately, calling his readers "brethren," which indicates he viewed them as believers in the Lord Jesus, loved them, had a close personal relationship with them, and cared for their spiritual well-being.

With tenderness and heartfelt concern for them, in humility and sincerity, he pleaded with them to "bear with" (listen to) him one more time. Some may have been ambivalent about remaining in the church because they were slothful in their walk with Christ and needed to be stirred up and reproved. So he gently and humbly asked them to pay conscientious, deliberate attention to his final exhortation without becoming exasperated.

The phrase *word of exhortation* refers to the exhortation given throughout the epistle. He implored them to stay committed to Christ; some had wavered due to persecution and the apostasy of others (cf. 2:1; 3:1, 12; 4:1, 11, 16; 6:1; 10:22, 35; 12:1; 13:1–3, 5, 7, 9, 13–17). Many needed to embrace the sound doctrines taught throughout Hebrews and leave the Jewish sacrificial system, with its ritual and ceremony.

While Hebrews might have seemed like an enormous, detailed letter to its readers, to its author it seemed like "few words." The phrase *few words* refers to the length of the epistle in view of the enormity of the issues with which it deals. The letter is a brief compendium of the vast subject matter relating to the importance of Christ and His ministry; volumes could have been written on the issues (cf. Jn. 21:25).

Abruptly, the author included a note concerning Timothy: "Know that our brother Timothy has been set free, with whom I shall see you if he comes shortly" (Heb. 13:23).

Timothy is the only Christian in Hebrews mentioned by name. A full understanding of this verse requires information the author did not share. He did say Timothy was "set free," meaning "released" or "set at liberty"—but from what? Most likely he was released from prison, but no New Testament reference confirms that the Timothy whom the apostle Paul mentored was ever in prison.

Since Timothy is called *our brother*, a phrase Paul used (2 Cor. 1:1; Col. 1:1; 1 Th. 3:2; Phile. 1), many believe it refers to him. Paul took that Timothy on his second missionary journey (Acts 16:1–3). He was with Paul in Corinth and was with him in Rome during Paul's first imprisonment. During Paul's second imprisonment, he asked Timothy to come to him quickly (2 Tim. 4:9). For these reasons, some commentators believe Paul wrote the epistle to the Hebrews.

Nevertheless, there is no conclusive evidence in the New Testament that Paul was the author.

Whoever Timothy was, he was not yet with the author, who hoped he would come soon and accompany him to visit the readers. Timothy's whereabouts is not known, nor is it known where the author resided while writing the letter. We do know he was not in prison.

A Farewell Postscript

The author closed the epistle with a word of greeting and grace: "Greet all those who rule over you, and all the saints. Those from Italy greet you. Grace be with you all" (Heb. 13:24–25).

First, he greeted the spiritual leaders with warmth and affection, giving them special recognition over those within the church. Second, he greeted the "saints," a common word for true believers—in this case, Hebrew Christians. Third, the Italians sent their greetings.

Commentators disagree as to the identity of the Italians. Where were they at the time this letter was written? Were they with the author? Were they inside or outside Italy? The verse gives no insight. It simply tells of their origin. They likely had some relationship with the Jewish believers or they would not have been mentioned. If they had no relationship with the readers, the author evidently explained the situation thoroughly to the Italians, who became deeply concerned for the readers' spiritual conditions.

The epistle closes with a blessing and benediction: "Grace be with you all. Amen" (v. 25). This benediction was common in the first century and often concluded other New Testament books (cf. Rom. 16:24; 2 Th. 3:18; Rev. 22:21). *Grace* can be defined as "that intrinsic quality of God's being or essence by which He is spontaneously favorable in His disposition and action to bestow unmerited favor, love, and mercy upon whom He chooses within undeserving humanity."

God's special grace to believers is manifested in their salvation, sanctification, serving, and suffering and is sufficient to strengthen them in every situation of life. This grace is marvelous, infinite, matchless, and freely bestowed on all who believe.

God's grace had been bestowed on and was experienced by the Jewish believers addressed in the epistle, resulting in their salvation. Now they needed to prove their commitment by living out their faith, which required being obedient to Christ and moving forward to maturity in Him. We must do likewise.

RECOMMENDED READING

Allen, D. L. *The New American Commentary: Hebrews*. Nashville, TN: B & H Publishing Group. Vol. 35. 2010.

Barclay, William. *The Letter to the Hebrews*. Rev. ed. The Daily Study Bible Series. Philadelphia, PA: Westminster, 1976.

Barnes, Albert. "Hebrews." *Notes on the New Testament Explanatory and Practical*. Grand Rapids, MI: Baker, 1977.

Bruce, F. F. *The Epistle to the Hebrews. The New International Commentary on the New Testament*. Grand Rapids, MI: Eerdmans, 1990.

Delitzsch, Franz. *Commentary on the Epistle to the Hebrews*. Translated by Thomas L. Kingsbury. 2 vols. Grand Rapids, MI: Eerdmans, 1871, 1952 reprint.

Ellingworth, Paul. *Commentary on Hebrews. The New International Greek Testament Commentary*. Grand Rapids, MI: Eerdmans, 1993.

English, E. Schuyler. *Studies in the Epistle to the Hebrews*. Neptune, NJ: Loizeaux Brothers, 1955.

Fruchtenbaum, Arnold G. *Ariel's Bible Commentary: The Messianic Jewish Epistles*. Tustin, CA: Ariel Ministries, 2005.

Gromacki, Robert. *Stand Bold in Grace*. Grand Rapids, MI: Baker Book House, 1984.

Guthrie, Donald. *The Letter to the Hebrews: An Introduction and Commentary*. The Tyndale New Testament Commentaries. Leicester, England: InterVarsity, 1983.

Guthrie, George. *The NIV Application Commentary: Hebrews*. Grand Rapids, MI: Zondervan Publishing House, 1998.

Hughes, Phillip E. *A Commentary on the Epistle to the Hebrews*. Grand Rapids, MI: Eerdmans, 1977.

Kent, Jr., Homer A. *The Epistle to the Hebrews*, 1972, reprint. Winona Lake, IN: BMH Books, 2002.

Lenski, R. C. H. *The Interpretation of the Epistle to the Hebrews and the Epistle of James*. Minneapolis, MN: Augsburg Publishing, 1966.

MacArthur, John. *Hebrews*. The MacArthur New Testament Commentary. Chicago, IL: Moody, 1983.

Newell, William. *Hebrews: Verse-by-Verse.* Chicago, IL: Moody, 1947.

O'Brien, Peter. *The Letter to the Hebrews.* The Pillar New Testament Commentary. Grand Rapids, MI: Eerdmans, 2010.

Pentecost, J. Dwight. *Faith That Endures.* Devotional notes by Ken Durham. Revised Edition. Grand Rapids, MI: Kregel, 2000.

Phillips, John. *Exploring Hebrews.* Chicago, IL: Moody, 1977.

Pink, Arthur. *An Exposition of Hebrews.* 3 vols. Grand Rapids, MI: Baker, 1954.

Thomas, W. H. Griffith. *Hebrews: A Devotional Commentary.* Grand Rapids, MI: Eerdmans, 1923.

Walvoord, John F. and Zuck, Roy B., editors. *The Bible Knowledge Commentary.* Wheaton, IL: Victor Books, 1983.

Westcott, B. F. *The Epistle to the Hebrews.* Grand Rapids, MI: Eerdmans, 1955 reprint.

Wiersbe, Warren W. *The Wiersbe Bible Commentary: New Testament.* Colorado Springs, CO: David C. Cook, 2007.

GENERAL INDEX

SCRIPTURE INDEX

OTHER BOOKS BY DAVID M. LEVY

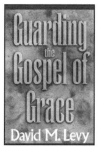

GUARDING THE GOSPEL OF GRACE
Contending for the Faith in the Face of Compromise
We often lack peace, joy, or victory in our walk with Christ because we're not clear how God's grace works in our lives. The books of Galatians and Jude are brought together in this marvelous work that explains grace, what can happen if you stray from it, and how to stay faithful.

JOEL: THE DAY OF THE LORD
What lies in store for the nations of the world? Learn what God has planned concerning the destiny of nations as they relate to Israel in the Day of the Lord. Illustrated chapter outlines and graphics give added insight into the timely and dynamic book of Joel, which surely is one of the most neglected and misinterpreted in the Bible.

MALACHI
Messenger of Rebuke and Renewal
Whatever the need—social, political, or religious—you'll find the answer in this verse-by-verse, nontechnical exposition that deals with contemporary issues while providing a comprehensive chronology of Israel's prophetic history.

REVELATION
Hearing the Last Word
Why is there so much uncertainty and disagreement about the last days? What can we know about the Antichrist? What is the order of end-times events? What about Israel? What will life be like in the Millennial Kingdom? This valuable resource will help you know what to expect as Earth's final hour approaches.

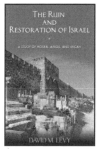

THE RUIN AND RESTORATION OF ISRAEL
A Study of Hosea, Amos, and Micah
An outstanding exposition that is as contemporary as today's news. Based on a literal-grammatical interpretation of Scripture, this book reveals the inerrancy of God's Word and shows how a covenant-keeping God chastens whom He loves but keeps His promises . . . forever.

THE TABERNACLE:
Shadows of the Messiah

Explore Israel's wilderness Tabernacle, the service of the priesthood, and the significance of the sacrifices. Excellent illustrations will open new vistas of biblical truth as ceremonies, sacrifices, and priestly service reveal the perfections of the Messiah.

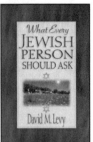

WHAT EVERY JEWISH PERSON SHOULD ASK

Can I know God? Why do I feel alienated from God? What can mitzvahs (good works) do for me? Is there really a Messiah? What decisions must I make about my spiritual life? If you need answers to life's most important questions, this excellent book is a must-read.

WHEN PROPHETS SPEAK OF JUDGMENT
Habakkuk, Zephaniah, Haggai

Is our nation on the brink of judgment? In this fascinating overview of Habakkuk, Zephaniah, and Haggai, you'll discover that the very conditions that led to Judah's downfall are all present in America today. This volume explores these conditions and challenges us to "redeem the time" as we move ever closer to the last days.

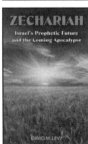

ZECHARIAH:
Israel's Prophetic Future and the Coming Apocalypse

Learn what lies ahead for Israel and the world. You'll see Israel's past successes and failures and how history repeats itself. Above all, you'll see into the prophetic future in magnificent detail, with end-times events culminating in the glorious reclamation of Israel followed by an era of genuine world peace when the Messiah reigns.